695

ORCHARDS

ORCHARDS
ORCHARDS
ORCHARDS

Stories by ANTON CHEKHOV

Plays by

MARIA IRENE FORNES

SPALDING GRAY

JOHN GUARE

DAVID MAMET

WENDY WASSERSTEIN

MICHAEL WELLER

SAMM-ART WILLIAMS

Alfred A. Knopf New York 1986

Library of Congress Cataloging-in-Publication Data
Chekhov, Anton Pavlovich, 1860–1904.
    Orchards.
    1. Chekhov, Anton Pavlovich, 1860–1904—Translations, English. 2. One-act plays, American. 3. American drama—20th century. I. Fornes, Maria Irene.
II. Title.
PG3456.A15 1986   891.73'3   85-45954
ISBN 0-394-55391-8
ISBN 0-394-74535-3 (pbk.)

Manufactured in the United States of America
FIRST EDITION

To ANNE CATTANEO,

who has the same initials

*The seven plays in this book
were originally commissioned by
The Acting Company,
a national repertory theater
on tour for the John F. Kennedy Center*

Producing Artistic Director
JOHN HOUSEMAN

Executive Producer
MARGOT HARLEY

Artistic Director
MICHAEL KAHN

"Commissioned" does not fully describe the unusual process through which the seven plays in this book were created.

The Acting Company, for which they were written, is the only permanent touring repertory ensemble in this country. Most of the fifty-nine plays it has performed in the past fifteen years in 298 American cities have been classics; because of the Company's traveling habits and insistence on repertory, it has had difficulty in attracting new plays, whose authors prefer to see them premiered in regular runs in New York or regional theaters.

In an attempt to find fresh contemporary material, the Company, under the stewardship of its Executive Producer, Margot Harley, came up with the notion of circulating a number of Chekhov's stories among a dozen of America's most successful young playwrights. The idea was not simply to adapt or dramatize the stories, but to use them as a cue for the creation of short theatrical pieces to be produced by the Company as part of its repertory season. The Company's dramaturg, Anne Cattaneo, read all of Chekhov's nearly one thousand stories and selected those she thought most compatible with the individual styles of the playwrights, whom she also selected.

Of the twelve writers approached, five declined, for valid personal or professional reasons; the rest came up with the variegated works contained in this volume. The plays have been rehearsed and presented by The Acting Company as part of its current tour. To date they have appeared in thirty-four cities, where in many cases audiences had their first opportunity to see works by the seven playwrights represented.

JOHN HOUSEMAN
New York, March 1986

CONTENTS

ORCHARDS

The Man in a Case

On the outskirts of the village of Mironitski, in a shed belonging to the bailiff Prokofi, some belated huntsmen were encamped for the night. There were two of them: the veterinary surgeon Ivan Ivanitch and the schoolteacher Burkin. Ivan Ivanitch had a rather strange, hyphenated surname, Tchimsha-Himalaiski, which did not suit him at all, and so he was known all over the province simply by his two Christian names. He lived on a stud farm near the town and had now come out hunting to get a breath of fresh air. Burkin, the schoolteacher, had long been at home in this neighborhood, for he came every year as the guest of Count P———.

They were not asleep. Ivan Ivanitch, a tall, spare old man with a long mustache, sat at the door of the shed, with the moon shining on him, smoking his pipe. Burkin lay inside on the hay and was invisible in the shadows.

They were telling stories. Among other things, they spoke of Mavra, the bailiff's wife, a healthy, intelligent woman who had never in her life been outside of her native village and who had never seen the town nor the railway; they remembered that she had sat beside the stove now for the last ten years, never going out into the street except after nightfall.

"There is nothing so very surprising in that," said Burkin.

"There are not a few people in this world who, like hermit crabs and snails, are always trying to retire into their shells. Perhaps this is a manifestation of atavism, a harking back to the time when man's forebears were not yet gregarious animals but lived alone in their dens, or perhaps it is simply one of the many phases of human character—who can say? I am not an anthropologist and it is not my business to meddle with such questions; I only mean to say that people like Mavra are not an uncommon phenomenon. Here! We don't have to go far to seek an illustration. Two months ago a certain Byelinkoff died in our town, a colleague of mine, a teacher of Greek. You must have heard of him. He was remarkable for one thing: no matter how fine the weather was, he always went out in galoshes, carrying an umbrella and wearing a warm, wadded overcoat. And his umbrella he always kept in a case and his watch in a case of gray chamois, and when he took out his penknife to sharpen a pencil that, too, was in a little case. Even his face seemed to be in a case, for he always kept it concealed behind the turned-up collar of his coat. He wore dark spectacles and a warm waistcoat, and he kept cotton wool in his ears and he had the hood raised whenever he got into a cab. In a word, one saw in this man a perpetual and irresistible longing to wrap some covering around himself—one might call it a case—which would isolate him from external impressions. Reality chafed and alarmed him and kept him in a state of perpetual apprehension, and it was, perhaps, to justify his timidity and his aversion to the present that he always exalted the past and things which had never existed. The ancient languages which he taught were at bottom the galoshes and umbrella behind which he hid himself from the realities of existence.

"'Oh, how musical, how beautiful is the Greek tongue!' he would cry with a beaming look, and, as if in proof of what he had said, he would half shut his eyes, hold up one finger, and pronounce the word 'anthropos'!

"And his opinions, too, Byelinkoff tried to confine in a case. Only bulletins and newspaper articles in which something was prohibited were clear to him. If he saw a bulletin forbidding the scholars to go out on the street after nine o'clock, or if he read an article enjoining him from carnal love, that was fixed and clear to him—and basta! For to him there was always an element of doubt, something unspoken and confused, concealed in license and liberty of action. When it was permitted to start a dramatic or reading club in the town he would shake his head and say softly:

"'That is all very well and very fine, but I shouldn't wonder if something unpleasant would come of it.'

"Every transgression and deviation from the right plunged him into dejection, although one wondered what business it was of his. If one of his colleagues came late to prayers, or if he heard rumors of some prank of the schoolboys, or if one of the lady superintendents was seen late at night with an officer, he would grow tremendously excited and always insist that something unpleasant would come of it. At the teachers' meetings he used to drive us absolutely mad by his prudence and his scruples and his absolutely caselike reflections. 'Oh,' he would cry, 'the boys and girls in the school behave so very badly and make such a noise in the classrooms! Oh, what if this should reach the governor's ears, and what if something unpleasant should come of it? If only Petroff could be expelled from the second class and Yegorieff from the fourth, how good it would be!' And what was the result? We would grow so oppressed with his sighing and his moaning and his dark spectacles on his white face that we would give in—give Petroff and Yegorieff bad-conduct marks, put them under arrest, and finally expel them.

"He had a strange habit—he used to make the tour of our rooms. He would come into a master's room and just sit and say nothing, as if he were looking for something. He would sit like that for an hour or so and then would go out. This he called 'keeping on good terms with his comrades,' but it was plainly a heavy burden for him to come and sit with us, and he only did it because he considered it his duty as our comrade. All of us teachers were afraid of him. Even the director feared him. Our teachers are all a thoughtful and thoroughly steady lot, brought up on Turgenieff and Shedrin, and yet this man, with his galoshes and his umbrella, held the whole school in the hollow of his hand for fifteen years. The whole school, did I say? The whole town! The ladies did not dare to get up little plays on Saturday evenings for fear he should hear of it, and the clergy were ashamed to eat meat and play cards in his presence. Under the influence of men like Byelinkoff the people of our town in the last ten or fifteen years have begun to fear everything. They are afraid of sending letters, of making acquaintances, of speaking aloud, of reading books, of helping or teaching the poor—"

Ivan Ivanitch coughed as a sign that he wanted to make a remark, but he first finished his pipe, then gazed at the moon, and then at last, pausing at intervals, said:

"Yes, they are thoughtful and steady; they read Shedrin and Turgenieff and others, and therefore they have submitted patiently—that is just it."

"Byelinkoff lived in the same house that I did," Burkin went on, "on the same floor. His door was opposite mine. We often met, and I was familiar with his domestic life. It was the same old story when he was at home. He wore a dressing gown and a nightcap and had shutters to his windows and bolts to his doors— a perfect array of restraints and restrictions and of 'oh-something-unpleasant-might-come-of-its.' Lenten fare was bad for the health, but to eat flesh was impossible because somebody might say that Byelinkoff did not keep the fasts; therefore he ate perch fried in butter, which was not Lenten fare, but neither could it be called meat. He would not keep a woman servant for fear that people might think ill of him, so he employed as a cook an old man named Afanasi, a besotted semi-idiot of sixty who had once been an officer's servant and could cook after a fashion. This Afanasi would stand at the door with folded arms, sigh deeply, and always mutter one and the same thing:

"'There's a whole lot of *them* out today!'

"Byelinkoff's bedroom was like a little box and curtains hung around his bed. When he went to sleep he would pull the blankets over his head. The room would be stuffy and hot, the wind rattle the closed doors and rumble in the stove, and sighs, ominous sighs, would be heard from the kitchen; and he would shake under his bedclothes. He was afraid that something unpleasant might come of it—that Afanasi might murder him, that burglars might break in. All night he would be a prey to alarming dreams, and in the morning, as we walked to the school together, he would be melancholy and pale, and one could see that the crowded school toward which he was going dismayed him and was repugnant to his whole being, and that it was burdensome for a man of his solitary disposition to be walking beside me.

"'There is so much noise in the classrooms,' he would say as if seeking an explanation of his depression.

"And think of it, this teacher of Greek, this man in a case, once very nearly got married!"

Ivan Ivanitch looked quickly around into the shed and said:

"You're joking!"

"Yes, he nearly got married, strange as it may appear. A new teacher of history and geography was appointed to our school, a certain Little Russian named Kovalenko. He did not come alone but brought his sister Varenka with him. He was young and tall and dark, with huge hands and a face from which it could be guessed that he possessed a bass voice. As a matter of fact, when he spoke his voice did sound as if it were coming out of a barrel—boo—boo—boo—. As for her, she was no longer young, thirty perhaps, but she was tall, too, and graceful, dark-eyed and red-cheeked—a sugar-plum of a girl, and so boisterous and jolly! She was always singing Little Russian songs and ha-ha-ing. At the slightest provocation she would break into loud peals of laughter—ha! ha! ha! I remember the first time we met the Kovalenkos; it was at a birthday party at the director's. Among the stern, tiresome teachers who go to birthday parties out of a sense of duty, we suddenly beheld a new Aphrodite risen from the waves, strolling about with her arms akimbo, laughing, singing, and dancing. She sang 'The Wind Blows' with feeling, and then another song, and then another, and fascinated us all, even Byelinkoff. He sat down beside her and said with a sweet smile:

"'The Little Russian tongue with its tenderness and pleasant sonorousness reminds me of ancient Greek.'

"This flattered her, and she began earnestly and with feeling to tell him that she had a farm in the province of Gadiatch, that her mamma lived there and that there were such pears and such melons there and such inns! Little Russians call gourds 'inns,' and make a soup out of the little red ones and the little blue ones that is 'so good, so good it is simply—awful!'

"We listened and listened, and the same thought suddenly crossed the minds of all of us.

"'How nice it would be to make a match between them!' said the director's wife to me quietly.

"For some reason we all remembered that our Byelinkoff was unmarried, and it now seemed strange to us that until this moment we had not noticed, had somehow quite overlooked this important detail in his life. By the way, how does he regard women? we asked ourselves. How does he solve this daily problem? This had not interested us before at all; perhaps we had not even entertained the idea that a man who wore galoshes in all weathers and slept behind bed curtains could possibly fall in love.

"'He is already long past forty, but she is thirty herself,' the director's wife expressed her opinion. 'I think she would marry him.'

"How many wrong and foolish deeds are committed in our country towns because we are bored! What need was there to have tried to marry off Byelinkoff, whom one could not even conceive of as being married? The director's wife and the inspector's wife and all the ladies of our school brightened and bloomed as if they had suddenly discovered the object of their existence. The director's wife takes a box at the theater, and, behold! in it sits Varenka waving a fan, radiant and happy, and beside her is

Byelinkoff, small and depressed, as if they had pulled him out of his room with a pair of pincers. I give an evening party, and the ladies insist that I shall invite both Byelinkoff and Varenka. In a word, the mills were grinding. It appeared that Varenka was not averse to marriage. It was not particularly cheerful for her living at her brother's, for they scolded and squabbled the day long. Here's a picture for you: Kovalenko is stalking down the street, a tall, lusty fellow in an embroidered shirt with his forelock hanging down over his forehead from under the brim of his cap. In one hand he carries a bundle of books, in the other a thick, knotted stick. Behind him walks his sister, also carrying books.

"'But you haven't read it, Mihailik!' she argues loudly. 'I tell you, I swear to you, you haven't read it at all!'

"'But I tell you I have read it!' shouts Kovalenko, rattling his stick on the sidewalk.

"'Oh, Lord have mercy, Mintchik! What are you getting so angry about; does it matter?'

"'But I tell you that I have read it!' shouts Kovalenko still louder.

"And at home, as soon as an outsider came in they would open fire at each other. A life like that was probably growing wearisome for her; she wanted a nook of her own; and then her age should be taken into account; at her years there's little time for picking and choosing—a woman takes what she can get, even if the man be a teacher of Greek. And, as a matter of fact, the majority of our young ladies will marry whom they can, only to get married. Well, be it as it may, Varenka began to show our Byelinkoff marked favor.

"And what about Byelinkoff? He called on the Kovalenkos as he did on the rest of us. He would go to their rooms and sit and say nothing. He would say nothing, but Varenka would sing 'The Wind Blows' for him, or gaze at him pensively out of her dark eyes, or suddenly break into peals of merry laughter—ha! ha! ha!

"In affairs of the heart, and especially in marriage, a large part is played by suggestion. Everyone—both the ladies and Byelinkoff's colleagues—all began to assure him that he ought to get married, that there was nothing for him to do but to marry. We all congratulated him and said all sorts of silly things with grave faces—that marriage was a serious step, and so forth. Besides that, Varenka was pretty and attractive; she was the daughter of a state councilor and owned a farm of her own; and, above all, she was the first woman who had treated him kindly and affectionately. His head was turned and he fancied that he really must marry."

"Now would have been the time to get rid of his galoshes and his umbrella," said Ivan Ivanitch.

"Will you believe it? That proved to be impossible. He put a photograph of Varenka on his table, and kept coming to me and talking to me about Varenka and family life, and about what a serious step marriage was; he was much at the Kovalenkos, but he did not change his way of living one atom. On the contrary, his resolve to get married affected him painfully; he grew thin and pale and seemed to shrink still further into his case.

"'I like Miss Varenka,' he said to me once with a wry smile, 'and I know every man ought to marry, but—all this has happened so suddenly; I must think it over a bit.'

"'What is there to think over?' I answered. 'Marry her! That's all there is to it.'

"'No, marriage is a serious step; one must first weigh the consequences and duties and responsibilities—so that nothing unpleasant shall come of it. All this worries me so that I can't sleep any more at night. And, to tell you the truth, I am alarmed: she and her brother have such a queer way of thinking; they reason somehow so strangely, and she has a very bold character. One might marry her and, before one knew it, get mixed up in some scandal.'

"And so he did not propose, but still kept putting it off, to the deep chagrin of the director's wife and of all of our ladies; he still kept weighing those duties and responsibilities, though he went walking every day with Varenka, thinking, no doubt, that this was due to a man placed as he was. He still kept coming to me to discuss family life.

"But in all probability he would have proposed at last, and one of those bad and foolish matches would have been consummated, as so many thousands are, simply because people have nothing better to do with themselves, had we not been suddenly over-whelmed by a colossal scandal.

"I must tell you that Varenka's brother could not abide Byelin-koff.

"'I can't understand,' he would say to us with a shrug of his shoulders, 'I can't imagine how you can stomach that sneak with his horrid face. Oh, friends, how can you live here? Your whole atmosphere here is stifling and nauseating. Are you instructors and teachers? No, you are sycophants, and this isn't a temple of learning; it's a detective office, stinking as sour as a police court. No, brothers, I'm going to stay here a little while longer, and then I'm going back to my farm to catch crawfish and teach young Little Russians. I am going, and you can stay here with your Judas.'

"Or else he would laugh and laugh till the tears rolled down his cheeks, now in a deep voice, now in a high squeaky one, and demand of me, spreading out his hands:

"'What does he sit in my room for? What is he after? He just sits and stares.'

"He even called Byelinkoff 'the spider,' and, of course, we avoided mentioning to him that his sister was thinking of marry-ing this 'spider.' When the director's wife once hinted to him that it would be a good idea to settle his sister with such a steady, universally respected man as Byelinkoff he frowned and growled:

"'That's none of my business. Let her marry a reptile if she likes. I can't endure interfering in other people's affairs.'

"And now listen to what followed. Some wag made a carica-ture of Byelinkoff in galoshes and cotton trousers, holding up an umbrella, with Varenka on his arm. Underneath was written:

'The Amorous Anthropos.' His expression was caught to perfection. The artist must have worked more nights than one, for every teacher in our school, every teacher in the seminary, and every official received a copy. Byelinkoff got one, too. The caricature made the most painful impression on him.

"We were coming out of our house together. It was on a Sunday, the first of May, and all of us, teachers and pupils, had agreed to meet at the school and from there walk out beyond the town into the woods. So we came out together, and his face was absolutely green; he looked like a thundercloud.

"'What bad, what unkind people there are!' he burst out, and his lips quivered.

"I really felt sorry for him. As we walked along, we suddenly saw Kovalenko riding toward us on a bicycle, followed by Varenka, also on a bicycle. She was scarlet and dusty, but merry and gay nevertheless.

"'We are going on ahead!' she cried. 'This weather is so glorious, so glorious, it's simply awful!'

"And they disappeared from view.

"Our Byelinkoff's face turned from green to white, and he seemed paralyzed. He stopped and looked at me.

"'Allow me, what do I see?' he asked. 'Or does my eyesight deceive me? Is it proper for schoolteachers and women to ride bicycles?'

"'What is there improper about it?' said I. 'Let them ride to their hearts' content.'

"'But how is it possible?' he shrieked, stupefied by my calmness. 'What are you saying?'

"And he was so shocked that he did not want to go on any farther, but turned and went home.

"Next day he rubbed his hands nervously all the time and trembled, and we could see from his face that he was not well. He left his work—the first time in his life that this had happened to him—and did not come to dinner. Toward evening he dressed himself warmly, although the weather was now quite summer-like, and crawled over to the Kovalenkos. Varenka was not at home; he found her brother alone.

"'Sit down,' said Kovalenko coldly and frowned. He looked sleepy; he had just had a nap after his dinner and was in a very bad humor.

"Byelinkoff sat for ten minutes in silence and then said:

"'I have come to you to relieve my mind. I am very, very much grieved. Some lampooner has made a picture of myself and a person who is near to us both in a ridiculous position. I consider it my duty to assure you that I have had nothing to do with this; I have never given any occasion for such a jest; I have always behaved with perfect propriety all the time.'

"Kovalenko sat moodily without saying a word. Byelinkoff waited a few minutes and then went on in a sad, low voice:

"'And I have something else to say to you. I have been a teacher for many years, and your career is just beginning: I consider it my duty as an older man to give you a word of warning. You ride the bicycle—now, this amusement is quite improper for a teacher of the young.'

"'Why?' asked Kovalenko in a deep voice.

"'Need I really explain that to you, Kovalenko? Isn't it obvious? If the master goes about on a bicycle, what is there left for the pupils to go about on? Only their heads! And if permission to do it has not been given in a bulletin, it must not be done. I was horrified yesterday. My head swam when I saw your sister—a woman or a girl on a bicycle—how terrible!'

"'What do you want, anyhow?'

"'I only want one thing: I want to caution you. You are a young man, the future lies before you, you must be very, very careful, or you will make a mistake. Oh, what a mistake you will make! You go about wearing embroidered shirts, you are always on the street with some book or other, and now you ride a bicycle! The director will hear of it; it will reach the ears of the trustees that you and your sister ride the bicycle—what is the use?'

"'It is nobody's business whether my sister and I ride the bicycle or not,' said Kovalenko, flushing deeply. 'And whoever interferes in my domestic and family affairs I will kick to the devil.'

"Byelinkoff paled and rose.

"'If you talk to me in that way I cannot continue,' he said. 'I must ask you never to refer to the heads of the school in that tone in my presence. You should have more respect for the authorities.'

"'Did I say anything against the authorities?' asked Kovalenko, glaring angrily at him. 'Please leave me alone, I am an honorable man, and I decline to talk to a person like you. I don't like sneaks!'

"Byelinkoff began nervously to bustle about and put on his things. You see, this was the first time in his life that he had heard such rudeness.

"'You can say what you like,' he cried as he stepped out of the hall onto the landing of the stairs. 'I must only warn you of one thing. Someone may have overheard our conversation and I shall have to report it to the director in its principal features, as it might be misinterpreted and something unpleasant might come of it. I shall be obliged to do this.'

"'To report it? Go ahead, report it!'

"Kovalenko seized him by the nape of the neck and pushed, and Byelinkoff tumbled downstairs with his galoshes rattling after him. The staircase was long and steep, but he rolled safely to the bottom, picked himself up, and touched his nose to make sure that his spectacles were all right. At the very moment of his descent Varenka had come in with two ladies; they stood at the foot of the stairs and watched him, and for Byelinkoff this was the most terrible thing of all. He would rather have broken his neck and both legs than to have appeared ridiculous; the whole town would now know it, the director, the trustees would hear of it—oh, something unpleasant would come of it! There would be another caricature, and the end of it would be that he would have to resign.

"As he picked himself up Varenka recognized him. When she caught sight of his absurd face, his wrinkled overcoat, and his galoshes, not knowing what had happened but supposing that he had fallen downstairs of his own accord, she could not control herself and laughed till the whole house rang:

"'Ha! ha! ha!'

"This pealing and rippling 'ha! ha! ha!' settled everything—it put an end to the wedding and to the earthly career of Byelinkoff.

"He did not hear what Varenka said to him; he saw nothing before his eyes. When he reached home he first took Varenka's picture off the table, then he went to bed and never got up again.

"Three days later Afanasi came to me and asked me whether he ought not to send for a doctor, as something was happening to his master. I went to see Byelinkoff. He was lying speechless behind his bed curtains, covered with a blanket, and when a question was asked him he only answered yes or no, and not another sound did he utter. There he lay, and about the bed roamed Afanasi, gloomy, scowling, sighing profoundly, and reeking of vodka like a taproom.

"A month later Byelinkoff died. We all went to his funeral, that is, the boys' and girls' schools and the seminary. As he lay in his coffin the expression on his face was timid and sweet, even gay, as if he were glad to be put in a case at last out of which he need never rise. Yes, he had attained his ideal! As if in his honor, the day of his funeral was overcast and rainy, and all of us wore galoshes and carried umbrellas. Varenka, too, was at the funeral and burst into tears when the coffin was lowered into the grave. I have noticed that Little Russian women always either laugh or cry, they know no middle state.

"I must confess that it is a great pleasure to bury such people as Byelinkoff. On our way back from the cemetery we all wore sober, Lenten expressions; no one wished to betray this feeling of pleasure, the same feeling that we used to have long, long ago in childhood when our elders went away from home and we could run about the garden for a few hours in perfect liberty. Oh, liberty, liberty! Even a hint, even a faint hope of its possibility lends the soul wings, does it not?

"We returned from the cemetery in a good humor, but before a week had elapsed our life was trickling on as sternly, as wearily, as senselessly as before; a life not prohibited in a bulletin and yet not quite permitted—no better than it had been!

"And, as a matter of fact, though we had buried Byelinkoff, how many more people in cases there were left! How many more there will be!"

"Yes, so, so, quite right," said Ivan Ivanitch, smoking his pipe.

"How many more there will be!" Burkin repeated.

The schoolmaster stepped out of the shed. He was a small man, fat, quite bald, with a black beard that reached almost to his waist; two dogs followed him out.

"What a moon! What a moon!" he exclaimed, looking up.

It was already midnight. To the right the whole village lay visible, its long street stretching away for three or four miles. Everything was wrapped in deep, peaceful slumber; not a movement, not a sound; it did not seem possible that nature could lie so silent. Peace fills the soul when one sees the broad street of a village on a moonlit night with its huts and its haystacks and its dreaming willows. It looks so gentle and beautiful and sad in its rest, screened by the shades of night from care and grief and toil. The stars, too, seem to be gazing at it with tenderness and emotion, and one feels that there is no evil in the world and that all is well. To the left the fields began at the edge of the village and were visible for miles down to the horizon; in all this broad expanse there was also neither movement nor sound.

"Yes, so, so, quite right," Ivan Ivanitch repeated. "But think how we live in town, so hot and cramped, writing unnecessary papers and playing vint—isn't that also a case? And isn't our whole life, which we spend among rogues and backbiters and stupid, idle women, talking and listening to nothing but folly—isn't that a case? Here! If you like I'll tell you a very instructive story."

"No, it's time to go to sleep," Burkin said. "Tomorrow!"

Both men went into the shed and lay down on the hay. They

had already covered themselves up and were half asleep when they suddenly heard light footsteps approaching—tip—tip. Somebody was walking by the shed. The footsteps went on and stopped, and in a minute came back again—tip—tip. The dogs growled.

"That was Mavra," said Burkin as the sound died away.

"One hears and sees all this lying," said Ivan Ivanitch, turning over on the other side. "Nobody calls one a fool for standing it all, for enduring insults and humiliations without daring to declare oneself openly on the side of free and honest people. One has to lie oneself and smile, all for a crust of bread, a corner to live in, and a little rank, which is not worth a penny—no, a man can't go on living like this."

"Oh, come, that's out of another opera, Ivan Ivanitch," said the schoolmaster. "Let's go to sleep!"

And ten minutes later Burkin was already asleep. But Ivan Ivanitch, sighing, still tossed from side to side, and at last got up and went out again and sat in the doorway smoking his pipe.

The Man in a Case

by

WENDY WASSERSTEIN

CHARACTERS

BYELINKOV

VARINKA

A small garden in the village of Mironitski. 1898.

BYELINKOV *is pacing. Enter* VARINKA *out of breath.*

BYELINKOV: You are ten minutes late.

VARINKA: The most amazing thing happened on my way over
here. You know the woman who runs the grocery store down
the road. She wears a black wig during the week, and a blond
wig on Saturday nights. And she has the daughter who married an engineer in Moscow who is doing very well thank you
and is living, God bless them, in a three-room apartment. But
he really is the most boring man in the world. All he talks
about is his future and his station in life. Well, she heard we
were to be married and she gave me this basket of apricots to
give to you.

BYELINKOV: That is a most amazing thing!

VARINKA: She said to me, Varinka, you are marrying the most
honorable man in the entire village. In this village he is the
only man fit to speak with my son-in-law.

BYELINKOV: I don't care for apricots. They give me hives.

VARINKA: I can return them. I'm sure if I told her they give you hives she would give me a basket of raisins or a cake.

BYELINKOV: I don't know this woman or her pompous son-in-law. Why would she give me her cakes?

VARINKA: She adores you!

BYELINKOV: She is emotionally loose.

VARINKA: She adores you by reputation. Everyone adores you by reputation. I tell everyone I am to marry Byelinkov, the finest teacher in the county.

BYELINKOV: You tell them this?

VARINKA: If they don't tell me first.

BYELINKOV: Pride can be an imperfect value.

VARINKA: It isn't pride. It is the truth. You are a great man!

BYELINKOV: I am the master of Greek and Latin at a local school at the end of the village of Mironitski.

(VARINKA *kisses him*)

VARINKA: And I am to be the master of Greek and Latin's wife!

BYELINKOV: Being married requires a great deal of responsibility. I hope I am able to provide you with all that a married man must properly provide a wife.

VARINKA: We will be very happy.

BYELINKOV: Happiness is for children. We are entering into a social contract, an amicable agreement to provide us with a secure and satisfying future..

VARINKA: You are so sweet! You are the sweetest man in the world!

BYELINKOV: I'm a man set in his ways who saw a chance to provide himself with a small challenge.

VARINKA: Look at you! Look at you! Your sweet round spectacles, your dear collar always starched, always raised, your perfectly pressed pants always creasing at right angles perpendicular to the floor, and my most favorite part, the sweet little galoshes, rain or shine, just in case. My Byelinkov, never taken by surprise. Except by me.

BYELINKOV: You speak about me as if I were your pet.

VARINKA: You are my pet! My little school mouse.

BYELINKOV: A mouse?

VARINKA: My sweetest dancing bear with galoshes, my little stale babka.

BYELINKOV: A stale babka?

VARINKA: I am not Pushkin.

BYELINKOV (*Laughs*):   That depends what you think of Pushkin.

VARINKA: You're smiling. I knew I could make you smile today.

BYELINKOV: I am a responsible man. Every day I have for breakfast black bread, fruit, hot tea, and every day I smile three times. I am halfway into my translation of the *Aeneid* from classical Greek hexameter into Russian alexandrines. In twenty years I have never been late to school. I am a responsible man, but no dancing bear.

VARINKA: Dance with me.

BYELINKOV: Now? It is nearly four weeks before the wedding!

VARINKA: It's a beautiful afternoon. We are in your garden. The roses are in full bloom.

BYELINKOV: The roses have beetles.

VARINKA: Dance with me!

BYELINKOV: You are a demanding woman.

VARINKA: You chose me. And right. And left. And turn. And right. And left.

BYELINKOV: And turn. Give me your hand. You dance like a school mouse. It's a beautiful afternoon! We are in my garden. The roses are in full bloom! And turn. And turn. (*Twirls* VARINKA *around*)

VARINKA: I am the luckiest woman!

(BYELINKOV *stops dancing*)

Why are you stopping?

BYELINKOV: To place a lilac in your hair. Every year on this day I will place a lilac in your hair.

VARINKA: Will you remember?

BYELINKOV: I will write it down. (*Takes a notebook from his pocket*) Dear Byelinkov, don't forget the day a young lady, your bride, entered your garden, your peace, and danced on the roses. On that day every year you are to place a lilac in her hair.

VARINKA: I love you.

BYELINKOV: It is convenient we met.

VARINKA: I love you.

BYELINKOV: You are a girl.

VARINKA: I am thirty.

BYELINKOV: But you think like a girl. That is an attractive attribute.

VARINKA: Do you love me?

BYELINKOV: We've never spoken about housekeeping.

VARINKA: I am an excellent housekeeper. I kept house for my family on the farm in Gadyatchsky. I can make a beetroot soup with tomatoes and aubergines which is so nice. Awfully awfully nice.

BYELINKOV: You are fond of expletives.

VARINKA: My beet soup, sir, is excellent!

BYELINKOV: Please don't be cross. I too am an excellent housekeeper. I have a place for everything in the house. A shelf for each pot, a cubby for every spoon, a folder for favorite recipes. I have cooked for myself for twenty years. Though my beet soup is not outstanding, it is sufficient.

VARINKA: I'm sure it's very good.

BYELINKOV: No. It is awfully, awfully not. What I am outstanding in, however, what gives me greatest pleasure, is preserving those things which are left over. I wrap each tomato slice I haven't used in a wet cloth and place it in the coolest corner of the house. I have had my shoes for seven years because I wrap them in the galoshes you are so fond of. And every night before I go to sleep I wrap my bed in quilts and curtains so I never catch a draft.

VARINKA: You sleep with curtains on your bed?

BYELINKOV: I like to keep warm.

VARINKA: I will make you a new quilt.

BYELINKOV: No. No new quilt. That would be hazardous.

VARINKA: It is hazardous to sleep under curtains.

BYELINKOV: Varinka, I don't like change very much. If one works out the arithmetic the final fraction of improvement is at best less than an eighth of value over the total damage caused by disruption. I never thought of marrying till I saw your eyes dancing among the familiar faces at the headmaster's tea. I assumed I would grow old preserved like those which are left over, wrapped suitably in my case of curtains and quilts.

VARINKA: Byelinkov, I want us to have dinners with friends and summer country visits. I want people to say, "Have you spent time with Varinka and Byelinkov? He is so happy now that they are married. She is just what he needed."

BYELINKOV: You have already brought me some happiness. But I never was a sad man. Don't ever think I thought I was a sad man.

VARINKA: My sweetest darling, you can be whatever you want! If you are sad, they'll say she talks all the time, and he is soft-spoken and kind.

BYELINKOV: And if I am difficult?

VARINKA: Oh, they'll say he is difficult because he is highly in-telligent. All great men are difficult. Look at Lermontov, Tchaikovsky, Peter the Great.

BYELINKOV: Ivan the Terrible.

VARINKA: Yes, him too.

BYELINKOV: Why are you marrying me? I am none of these things.

VARINKA: To me you are.

BYELINKOV: You have imagined this. You have constructed an elaborate romance for yourself. Perhaps you are the great one. You are the one with the great imagination.

VARINKA: Byelinkov, I am a pretty girl of thirty. You're right, I am not a woman. I have not made myself into a woman because I do not deserve that honor. Until I came to this town to visit my brother I lived on my family's farm. As the years passed I became younger and younger in fear that I would never marry. And it wasn't that I wasn't pretty enough or sweet enough, it was just that no man ever looked at me and saw a wife. I was not the woman who would be there when he came home. Until I met you I thought I would lie all my life and say I never married because I never met a man I loved. I will love you, Byelinkov. And I will help you to love me. We deserve the life everyone else has. We deserve not to be different.

BYELINKOV: Yes. We are the same as everyone else.

VARINKA: Tell me you love me.

BYELINKOV: I love you.

VARINKA (*Takes his hands*): We will be very happy. I am very strong. (*Pauses*) It is time for tea.

BYELINKOV: It is too early for tea. Tea is at half past the hour.

VARINKA: Do you have heavy cream? It will be awfully nice with apricots.

BYELINKOV: Heavy cream is too rich for teatime.

VARINKA: But today is special. Today you placed a lilac in my hair. Write in your note pad. Every year we will celebrate with apricots and heavy cream. I will go to my brother's house and get some.

BYELINKOV: But your brother's house is a mile from here.

VARINKA: Today it is much shorter. Today my brother gave me his bicycle to ride. I will be back very soon.

BYELINKOV: You rode to my house by bicycle! Did anyone see you?

VARINKA: Of course. I had such fun. I told you I saw the grocery store lady with the son-in-law who is doing very well thank you in Moscow, and the headmaster's wife.

BYELINKOV: You saw the headmaster's wife!

VARINKA: She smiled at me.

BYELINKOV: Did she laugh or smile?

VARINKA: She laughed a little. She said, "My dear, you are very progressive to ride a bicycle." She said you and your fiancé Byelinkov must ride together sometime. I wonder if he'll take off his galoshes when he rides a bicycle.

BYELINKOV: She said that?

VARINKA: She adores you. We had a good giggle.

BYELINKOV: A woman can be arrested for riding a bicycle. That is not progressive, it is a premeditated revolutionary act. Your brother must be awfully, awfully careful on behalf of your behavior. He has been careless—oh so careless—in giving you the bicycle.

VARINKA: Dearest Byelinkov, you are wrapping yourself under curtains and quilts! I made friends on the bicycle.

BYELINKOV: You saw more than the headmaster's wife and the idiot grocery woman.

VARINKA: She is not an idiot.

BYELINKOV: She is a potato-vending, sausage-armed fool!

VARINKA: Shhhh! My school mouse. Shhh!

BYELINKOV: What other friends did you make on this bicycle?

VARINKA: I saw students from my brother's classes. They waved and shouted, "Anthropos in love! Anthropos in love!!"

BYELINKOV: Where is that bicycle?

VARINKA: I left it outside the gate. Where are you going?

BYELINKOV (*Muttering as he exits*):   Anthropos in love, anthropos in love.

VARINKA: They were cheering me on. Careful, you'll trample the roses.

BYELINKOV (*Returning with the bicycle*):   Anthropos is the Greek singular for man. Anthropos in love translates as the Greek and Latin master in love. Of course they cheered you. Their instructor, who teaches them the discipline and contained beauty of the classics, is in love with a sprite on a bicycle. It is a good giggle, isn't it? A very good giggle! I am returning this bicycle to your brother.

VARINKA: But it is teatime.

BYELINKOV: Today we will not have tea.

VARINKA: But you will have to walk back a mile.

BYELINKOV: I have my galoshes on. (*Gets on the bicycle*) Varinka, we deserve not to be different. (*Begins to pedal. The bicycle doesn't move*)

VARINKA: Put the kickstand up.

BYELINKOV: I beg your pardon.

VARINKA (*Giggling*):   Byelinkov, to make the bicycle move, you must put the kickstand up.

(BYELINKOV *puts it up and awkwardly falls off the bicycle as it moves*)

(*Laughing*) Ha ha ha. My little school mouse. You look so funny! You are the sweetest dearest man in the world. Ha ha ha!

(*Pause*)

BYELINKOV: Please help me up. I'm afraid my galosh is caught.

VARINKA (*Trying not to laugh*):   Your galosh is caught! (*Explodes in laughter again*) Oh, you are so funny! I do love you so. (*Helps* BYELINKOV *up*) You were right, my pet, as always. We don't need heavy cream for tea. The fraction of improvement isn't worth the damage caused by the disruption.

BYELINKOV: Varinka, it is still too early for tea. I must complete two stanzas of my translation before late afternoon. That is my regular schedule.

VARINKA: Then I will watch while you work.

BYELINKOV: No. You had a good giggle. That is enough.

VARINKA: Then while you work I will work too. I will make lists of guests for our wedding.

BYELINKOV: I can concentrate only when I am alone in my house. Please take your bicycle home to your brother.

VARINKA: But I don't want to leave you. You look so sad.

BYELINKOV: I never was a sad man. Don't ever think I was a sad man.

VARINKA: Byelinkov, it's a beautiful day, we are in your garden. The roses are in bloom.

BYELINKOV: Allow me to help you on to your bicycle. (*Takes* VARINKA'*s hand as she gets on the bike*)

VARINKA: You are such a gentleman. We will be very happy.

BYELINKOV: You are very strong. Good day, Varinka.

(VARINKA *pedals off.* BYELINKOV, *alone in the garden, takes out his pad and rips up the note about the lilac, strews it over the garden, then carefully picks up each piece of paper and places them all in a small envelope as lights fade to black*)

Vint

One nasty autumn night Andrey Stepanovich Peresolin was being driven home from the theater. As he rode along he meditated on the fact that theaters could be such useful institutions if only the plays produced there were of an improving nature. He was driving past the Provincial Administration building when he stopped his utilitarian meditations and directed his gaze to the windows of the building where, to use the language of poets and skippers, he was at the helm. Two windows in the secretaries' room were brightly lit.

"Can it be they're still busy with that report?" Peresolin wondered. "There are four of them there, and the fools haven't finished yet! Heaven help us, people may think I keep them working all night. I'll go and hurry them up. Stop, Gury!"

Peresolin climbed out of the carriage and walked toward the building. The front door was locked, but the back door had a broken latch and was open. Peresolin took advantage of this, and a moment later he was standing at the entrance to the secretaries' room. The door was ajar and Peresolin, looking in, was amazed at the sight that met his eyes. At the table, on which lay a pile of large sheets covered with figures and which was lit by a couple of lamps, sat four government clerks playing cards. Tense, immobile, their faces green with the reflection of the lampshades, they resembled the gnomes of the fairy tales or, God forbid, counterfeiters. . . . The game they were playing made them appear even more mysterious. To judge from their behavior and the card terms that they shouted from time to time, they were playing vint. To judge from everything else that Peresolin heard, however, they were occupied neither with vint nor any other card game. It was something unheard-of, weird, fantastic. Peresolin recognized the clerks to be Serafim Zvizdulin, Stepan Kulakevich, Yeremey Nedoyekhov, and Ivan Pisulin.

"How are you leading, you Dutch devil?" Zvizdulin shouted angrily, glaring with exasperation at his partner opposite. "What kind of a lead is that? I had Dorofeyev, protected, in my hand, besides Shepelev and wife, and Yerlakov. You lead Kofeikin. And here we've lost two tricks! And you, you cabbage head, you should have led Pogankin!"

"What good would it have done?" his partner snapped. "Suppose I had led Pogankin—Ivan here has Peresolin in his hand."

"They're bandying my name about," Peresolin said to himself, shrugging his shoulders. "I can't make head or tail of it."

Pisulin dealt again, and the players continued:

"State Bank."

"Two Treasury."

"Got no ace."

"You haven't an ace? Hmm! Two Provincial Administration. If I lose, then I lose, what the devil! Before, because I led Ministry of Education, I was cleaned out, and now I'll get into hot water with Provincial Administration. I don't give a damn."

"Small slam, thanks to my Ministry of Education!"

"I don't get it," whispered Peresolin.

"I lead State Councilor. Vanya, throw off a wee Titular Councilor or a Provincial Secretary."

"Why throw off a Titular? Anyway, we'll do something with Peresolin yet."

"We'll knock the stuffing out of Peresolin. We've got Rybnikov. You'll lose three tricks. Well, bring out Peresolin's missus: don't hide the bitch in your cuff."

"That's my wife they're talking about," thought Peresolin. "I don't get it."

Peresolin could not bear to remain in the dark any longer; he swung the door open and entered the room. If the devil himself, with horns and tail, had materialized before the clerks, he wouldn't have astonished and terrified them as their Chief astonished and terrified them. If their colleague who had died the previous year had appeared there and said in a spectral voice: "Follow me, bless you, to the place prepared for rascals," and if he had breathed upon them the chill of the grave, they would not have blanched as they did when they recognized Peresolin. Fright gave Nedoyekhov a nosebleed. Kulakevich felt a drumming in his right ear, and his tie came loose of itself. The clerks threw down their cards, rose slowly, and after glancing at one another, fixed their gaze on the floor. For a moment silence reigned in the room.

"So that's the way you copy the report!" Peresolin began. "Now I understand why you like working on the report so much. What were you doing just now?"

"It was just for a minute or two, your Excellency," muttered Zvizdulin. "We were just looking at the cards . . . resting. . . ."

Peresolin approached the table and slowly shrugged his shoulders. On the table lay not ordinary cards, but photographs of the usual size removed from their cardboard mats and pasted on playing cards. There were many such. Looking them over, Peresolin recognized himself, his wife, a number of his subordinates and acquaintances.

"It's absurd! How do you play?"

"We didn't invent this, your Excellency . . . God forbid! We just picked it up . . ."

"Explain it to me, Zvizdulin. How were you playing, anyway? I saw it all, and I heard how you topped me with Rybnikov. What are you fidgeting about, friend? I'm not going to eat you. Go ahead, tell me."

For a while Zvizdulin held back, in embarrassment and some fear. Finally, when Peresolin lost his temper, snorted, and got red with impatience, he obeyed. Having collected the cards and shuffled them, he laid them out on the table and began his explanation:

"Each picture, your Excellency, just like a card, has its meaning . . . its value. . . . As in a regular pack, there are fifty-two cards and four suits. Treasury officials are hearts, Provincial Administration officials are clubs, those in the Ministry of Education are diamonds, and the employees of the State Bank are spades. Well, sir . . . Actual Councilors of State we count as aces, State Councilors as kings, their spouses as queens, Collegiate Councilors are jacks, Court Councilors are tens, and so on down. For instance, I, here's my card, I'm a three, since I am a Provincial Secretary."

"Well, think of that! That makes me an ace?"

"Ace of clubs. And her Excellency is queen of clubs."

"Hmm, that's original! Well, let's have a game. I'll see what it's like."

Peresolin took off his overcoat and, smiling skeptically, sat down at the table. At his behest, the clerks, too, sat down, and the game commenced.

When, at seven o'clock in the morning, Nazar, the porter, came in to sweep the secretaries' room, he was amazed. So striking was the picture he beheld when he entered with his mop that he still remembers it, even when he lies stupefied with drink. Peresolin, pale and sleepy-looking, his hair mussed, was standing in front of Nedoyekhov, whom he had buttonholed, and was saying:

"Get it into your head that you couldn't lead Shepelev if you knew that in my hand I had myself, and the next three in the same suit. Zvizdulin had Rybnikov and wife, three high school teachers, and my wife; and Kulakevich had State Bank people

and three small ones from the Provincial Administration. You
should have led Kryshkin! You should have paid no attention to
the fact that they led the Treasury. They're foxy."

"Your Excellency, I led a Titular Councilor because I thought
that they had an Actual Councilor of State."

"Oh, my boy, that's no way to think! That's no game! Only
shoemakers play that way. Consider: when Kulakevich led a
Court Councilor you should have thrown off Ivan Ivanovich
Grenlandsky, because you knew that he had Natalya Dmitryevna
and two more in that suit, and Yegor Yegorych besides. You
ruined everything! Here, I'll prove it to you. Sit down, gentlemen, we'll play another rubber."

And sending away the astounded Nazar, the company sat
down and resumed the game.

Vint

by

DAVID MAMET

CHARACTERS

PORTER

COMMISSIONER PERSOLIN

ZVISDULIN

KULAKEVITCH

NEDKUDOV

PSIULIN

A PORTER *and* COMMISSIONER PERSOLIN, *walking down the corridors of power, late at night.*

PORTER: You wish the coach to wait, your Excellency?

PERSOLIN: I've told him to. I just need the one file.

PORTER: I may say so, sir. It must be important, to drag you in so late.

PERSOLIN: It is, yes. It's for the Quarterly Report.

PORTER: Oh, yes, sir. Tomorrow's the day.

PERSOLIN: What's that I hear? (*Pauses*)

PORTER: Clerks, sir.

PERSOLIN: Clerks. (*Pauses*)

PORTER: Your clerks.

PERSOLIN: They're still here?

PORTER: Yessir.

PERSOLIN: They stayed to work on the report. God bless *them*. What is a man without his staff?

PORTER: As you say, Commissioner Persolin.

PERSOLIN: I think a commendation is in order here. (*Hands a slip of paper to* PORTER) Fetch me this file. (PORTER *goes off.* PERSOLIN *goes up to a door behind which we hear the clerks muttering. Speaks to himself*) My bully, bully boys . . .

ZVISDULIN (*Behind the door*):   My bid. An Interoffice Clerk.

KULAKEVITCH: Two Treasury.

PERSOLIN (*To himself*):   Two Treasury what?

NEDKUDOV: No, may we stop a moment, please?

ZVISDULIN: Finish the bidding. Eh?

PERSOLIN (*To himself*):   The bidding?

NEDKUDOV: Finish it *nothing*. Not at all. My partner leads an Interoffice Clerk, and then two *Treasury* . . . ?

KULAKEVITCH: It was my bid.

PERSOLIN (*To himself*):   What's going on here?

NEDKUDOV: All that I . . .

PSIULIN: It's his *bid*. Let it stand. When it's *your* bid, then *you* bid.

NEDKUDOV: All right . . . all right . . .

(*Pause*)

PSIULIN: It's your bid.

NEDKUDOV: All right . . . two Treasury, and I raise . . . Vrazhansky.

KULAKEVITCH: Fine. Vrazhansky.

NEDKUDOV: Your bid . . . ?

PSIULIN: Madame Persolin.

    (PERSOLIN *bursts in*)

PERSOLIN: What's going on here? (*Pauses*) I said, what's going
on here?

KULAKEVITCH: Sir . . .

PERSOLIN: Yes. Sir. What? Come on. . . . Surprised to find you
here, thought you were for once doing the work you're *paid* to,
what do I . . . bandying the name of my wife. (*Pauses*) Now.

    (*Pause*)

NEDKUDOV: Commissioner Persolin.

PERSOLIN: Now: What does this mean?

    (*Pause*)

ZVISDULIN: We . . .

PERSOLIN: Yes. What what what? Up all night . . . finish the
report—I come in. I . . . *What are you doing?*

KULAKEVITCH: We were playing cards.

    (*Pause*)

PERSOLIN: Playing cards. And bandying the name of my wife.

ZVISDULIN: Yes. As you see . . . playing cards and . . .

PERSOLIN: Ignorant as I am it seems to me those are not cards
but Identity Dossiers.

    (*Pause*)

NEDKUDOV: Yes, sir, that's what they are.

PERSOLIN: That's what they are.

NEDKUDOV: Yes. Sir.

PERSOLIN: So what is it I'm privy to? In this perversion? In this
. . . this unauthorized use of . . . Treason? I would have
thought you lacked the initiative. But. No. Unauthorized files,
you . . .

KULAKEVITCH: We assure you, sir. We. We were only playing
vint.

PERSOLIN: Playing vint.

KULAKEVITCH: Yessir.

(*Pause*)

PERSOLIN: With Identity Dossiers.

KULAKEVITCH: Yes, sir.

PERSOLIN: And how *is* that? Well. Let me *profit* from it, *please*.

(*Pause*)

NEDKUDOV (*To* KULAKEVITCH):   *You* go.

(*Pause*)

KULAKEVITCH: Um. Each name, you see, your Excellency . . .

PERSOLIN: Yes . . .

KULAKEVITCH: Each name is like a card. Just like a regular deck.
Four suits. Fifty-two cards. Men of the Treasury are hearts,
the Provincial Administrators clubs, the State Bank spades,
the Ministry of Education . . . and so on, you see . . . State
Councilors are aces, Assistant State Councilors . . .

NEDKUDOV: It's very easy, sir . . . and down the line. Collegiate
Councilors jacks, their wives are queens . . .

PERSOLIN: . . . wives of the Collegiate Councilors . . .

KULAKEVITCH: . . . are queens . . . Court Councilors are tens,
and so on. I . . . here's *my* card: Stepan Kulakevitch: three.

PERSOLIN: You're a three.

KULAKEVITCH: Three of, yessir, the three of clubs. And Zvis-dulin, here, he's a—

PERSOLIN: What am I?

(*Pause*)

ZVISDULIN: Ace of clubs.

(*Pause*)

PERSOLIN: I'm the ace of clubs.

KULAKEVITCH: Yessir.

PERSOLIN: And my wife?

KULAKEVITCH: Is the queen of clubs.

PERSOLIN: You said the queen was the spouse of the jack.

ZVISDULIN: As the jack in Provincial has no wife . . .

PERSOLIN: Ah.

KULAKEVITCH (*Confidentially*):   It's Mosischev . . .

PERSOLIN: Yes, I know.

ZVISDULIN: . . . and neither the king, we took the liberty . . .

KULAKEVITCH: . . . and meant no disre—

PERSOLIN: Yes, yes, yes, and so my wife's the queen of clubs.

(*Pause*)

NEDKUDOV: Yessir.

PERSOLIN: And as I came in she'd just—

PSIULIN: I'd had the honor to *bid* her.

NEDKUDOV: As you came in she'd just taken a trick over two Treasury half-councilors.

PERSOLIN: She did.

NEDKUDOV: Yes.

PERSOLIN: And who were they?

KULAKEVITCH (*Checks*):   Ostopchin and Brot.

(*Pause*)

PERSOLIN: And she took that trick.

KULAKEVITCH: Yes.

NEDKUDOV: You see, he led the Interoffice Clerk. Why? *Why*, I said . . .

KULAKEVITCH: I countered with the Treasury.

PERSOLIN: Why make the diamonds vulnerable?

NEDKUDOV: That's what *I* said. That's what *I* said!

PERSOLIN: And so you've got to come back with my wife.

NEDKUDOV: Wasted a perfectly good queen. With all resp—

PERSOLIN: No, you're quite right. Wasted. Yes. Who taught you to play? He leads who? The Interoffice . . . ?

ZVISDULIN: Brulin and Baschenko.

PERSOLIN: He leads Brulin. Brulin *and* Baschenko?

ZVISDULIN: Yes.

PERSOLIN: *Why?*

ZVISDULIN: To force—

PERSOLIN: You know . . . you're laying the whole Ministry open to—

NEDKUDOV: That's what *I* said.

PERSOLIN: Look—look—can I get in?

KULAKEVITCH: Sir, we'd be honored to—

NEDKUDOV: Give him the cards.

ZVISDULIN: Deal him in.

(PERSOLIN *is dealt in*)

PERSOLIN: All right. Now: let's go back to *you*.

PSIULIN: I bid your wife.

PERSOLIN: My bid?

PSIULIN: Yes.

PERSOLIN: All right. Grand Court Councilor, I give you: Ivan
Dimich Grelandsky.

(*Pause*)

NEDKUDOV: Brilliant.

PERSOLIN: Well, you *see* . . . ?

NEDKUDOV: Brilliant.

PERSOLIN: If he comes out with Education . . .

KULAKEVITCH: Yes . . .

PERSOLIN: What do I have? Look: let's play this hand open. I
have *Grelandsky* . . . Paschin . . .

NEDKUDOV: Yes.

(*The* PORTER *sticks his head in*)

PORTER: Excellency, I have the file.

PERSOLIN (*Brushing him off*):   Just . . . just . . . just . . .

NEDKUDOV: Finish the hand: the man bid Grelandsky.

KULAKEVITCH: All right. Grelandsky, and . . . has Potkin fallen?

PSIULIN: No, we're void in Education.

PORTER: Excellency . . . ?.

PERSOLIN (*Sternly*): Will you *please* . . . ?

KULAKEVITCH: All right. Grelandsky and . . . um . . . um . . .

NEDKUDOV: No prompting.

KULAKEVITCH: And . . . um . . .

PERSOLIN: Just bid, will you?

KULAKEVITCH: All right, I . . .

PERSOLIN: What are you, working by the *hour*? Come *on*. Come on!

Drowning

A Little Scene

The quay of a wide, navigable river is bustling with the activity usual there on a summer afternoon. The loading and unloading of barges is in full swing. The air is thick with ceaseless cursing and the hissing of steamers. "Chrrrly-chrrrly" moan the windlasses. There is a heavy smell of smoked fish and pitch.

An agent of the Scribbler shipping firm is sitting at the very edge of the water, waiting for a consignor. He is approached by a stocky individual with a terribly ravaged, bloated face, who is dressed in a ragged jacket and patched striped trousers. He wears a faded cap with a broken visor and the mark left by a long since vanished badge. His tie has parted from his collar and rides up on his neck.

"My compliments, sir merchant!" the individual ejaculates hoarsely, with a military salute. "Evviva! How would you like to see a drowned man, Your Worship?"

"Where is your drowned man?" asks the agent.

"Actually, there is no drowned man, but I can impersonate him for you. A leap into the water and—and a drowning man perishes before your eyes. The tableau is not tragic but ironical, in view of its comic features. . . . Allow me to perform for you, sir merchant!"

"I'm no merchant."

"I regret my mistake. *Mille pardons* . . . Nowadays merchants dress like everybody else, so that Noah himself wouldn't be able to tell the clean from the unclean. But it's all the better that you are a member of the educated classes. . . . We shall understand each other. I, too, belong to the gentry. I am the son of a commissioned officer, and at one time I was accorded the rank of the fourteenth degree.* . . . And so, milord, a master of arts is offering you his services. . . . One leap into the water, and there is a tableau before you."

"No, thank you."

"If considerations of a material nature trouble you, I hasten to reassure you. . . . For you the fee will be a small one. . . . Two rubles for drowning myself with my boots on, one ruble—without them."

"Why the difference?"

"Because boots are the most expensive item of attire, and the hardest to dry. Ergo, you will allow me to earn an honest ruble?"

"No, I'm not a merchant, and I don't fancy such thrills."

"Hmm . . . I'm afraid that you are laboring under a false impression. You seem to think that I'm offering you something crude and vulgar, but I assure you, sir, it'll be nothing but humorous and satirical. You will smile an extra smile, and that's all. Isn't it funny to see a man fully dressed battling with the waves? And besides, you will give me a chance to earn an honest ruble."

"Instead of impersonating a drowning man, you ought to do some useful work."

"Useful work . . . and what work would that be? No one will give me employment in keeping with my station, because I'm inclined to alcoholism, and further, for that you have to be able to pull wires. And a man of my rank cannot bring himself to accept manual labor."

"To hell with your rank."

---

* The lowest degree in the bureaucratic hierarchy. *Translator's note.*

"What do you mean: to hell with it?" the man says with a smirk, throwing back his head haughtily. "If a bird understands that it's a bird, how can a person of rank fail to understand what he is? I may be impoverished, yes, ragged, destitute, but I have my purr-rride—I'm proud of my birth!"

"Yet your pride does not prevent you from swimming around fully dressed."

"I blush! Your remark has its ingredient of bitter truth. One can see that you are a person of culture. But before casting a stone at a sinner, hear me out. True, there are many individuals among us who forget their dignity and allow ignorant merchants to plaster their heads with mustard, or who will smear themselves with soot in the public baths to masquerade as the devil, or even put on women's clothes and perform all sorts of indecencies: but me—you won't find me doing anything like that. No matter how much money a merchant offers me, I will not permit him to plaster my head with mustard or any other less ignoble substance. But I see nothing shameful in impersonating a drowning man. Water is a wet, clean object. Submersion will not soil you, quite the contrary: it cleanses you. Nor is medicine against it. However, if it doesn't suit you, I can reduce the fee. . . . So be it, I'll drown myself with my boots on for one ruble."

"No, I'm not interested."

"But why not, sir?"

"I don't care about it, that's all."

"You should see me gurgle and gasp in the water. There's no man the length of this river who drowns better than I do. If Messrs. the doctors could see the face I make when I'm dead, they'd give me a medal. Well, just for you I'll bring it down to sixty kopecks. You're the first customer, I'll do it for you cheap. I wouldn't perform even for three rubles if it were anybody else, but I see by your face that you are a kind gentleman. . . . The educated I charge less."

"Please leave me alone!"

"Just as you say. Freedom for the free, salvation for the saved.

Only you're making a mistake. Another day you'll be ready to spend ten rubles, but you won't find a drowning man. . . ."

The individual sits down not far from the agent and, breathing heavily, begins to rummage in his pockets.

"Hmm . . . damn it . . ." he mumbles. "Where's my tobacco? I must have left it on the dock. . . . I got carried away arguing with an officer about politics, and I mislaid my cigarette case. There is a cabinet crisis in England now. People are queer! I wonder, could you let me have a cigarette, Your Honor?"

The agent hands him a cigarette. At that moment a merchant, the consignor for whom the agent has been waiting, appears on the scene. The individual leaps to his feet, hides the cigarette in his hand, and gives a military salute.

"My compliments, Your Worship!" he brings out hoarsely. "Evviva!"

"Ah, it's you!" says the agent to the merchant. "You've kept me waiting quite a while. And this character here has been wearing me out. He keeps pestering me by offering to perform. For sixty kopecks he undertakes to impersonate a drowning man. . . ."

"Sixty kopecks? That's overcharging, brother," says the merchant, turning to the derelict. "Twenty-five kopecks is the outside price. Why, the other day thirty men acted out a whole shipwreck for us, and it didn't cost us more than a fiver, and you—you ask sixty kopecks! Well, I'll give you thirty kopecks!"

The individual puffs out his cheeks and smirks contemptuously.

"Thirty kopecks! . . . Nowadays you have to pay that much for a head of cabbage, and you want a drowned man for the same price. That won't do."

"Never mind, then. I have no time to bother with you."

"Well, all right, since you're the first customer. Only don't tell the other merchants that I've done it so cheaply."

The man takes off his boots and, lifting his chin, approaches the water with a frown and clumsily throws himself in. There is the thud of a heavy body falling into the water. Coming to the surface, he waves his arms absurdly, kicks his legs, and tries to force an expression of panic. But, instead of showing panic, his face twitches with cold.

"Drown! Drown!" the merchant shouts. "You've done enough swimming—drown!"

The man blinks his eyes and, spreading his arms wide, sinks under the water. That's the end of the performance. Having "drowned," the individual climbs out of the water and, on receiving his thirty kopecks, walks off, wet and shivering with cold.

Drowning

by

MARIA IRENE FORNES

CHARACTERS

PEA

ROE

STEPHEN

A café, probably in Europe. PEA and ROE sit at a table. PEA to the right, ROE to the left. It is late afternoon. There is a lot of olive green in the air and the trimmings are olive green enamel. PEA's and ROE's heads are large and shapeless, like potatoes. Their skin is dark. Their flesh is shiny and oily. Their eyes are reddish and watery. They have warts on their faces and necks. Their bodies are also like potatoes. PEA wears an olive hat, a beige jacket, and greenish-brown pants. ROE wears a brown hat and a brown suit. When they breathe their bodies sweat. Their skin and general shape resemble those of seals or sea lions. There is a folded news-paper on the table. PEA looks at it.

PEA: My God, what is it?

ROE: It's a newspaper.

PEA: It is beautiful. (ROE *nods*) May I touch it? (ROE *nods*. PEA *touches the paper. A tear rolls down his face*) This must be made by a person.

ROE: Yes, many of them. They put out a new one each day.

(PEA *lifts the corner of the first page. He gasps. He puts the palm of his hand on the paper tenderly. He takes his hand off and looks at it again*)

PEA (*Pointing*):   Is this not a woman?

ROE: Yes.

PEA (*Pointing*):   And what is this?

(ROE *looks*)

ROE: A snowdrift. (PEA *looks at* ROE) It is snow that has been blown by the wind. (*Looks at the caption*) It's seven feet high.

PEA: It is very high.

ROE: Yes.

PEA: What is snow?

ROE: Snow is rain that freezes as it falls to the ground. It freezes with the cold. It becomes white and it is not liquid. It is more like powder. (*Pointing*) You see here? They have made a snowman.

PEA: A man?

ROE: Not a real man. They have packed the snow and shaped it so it resembles a man.

PEA: How awkward.

ROE: Why is it awkward?

PEA: Oh, isn't it?

ROE: Well no, I think it's very well made.

PEA: Oh yes! It's very well made.

ROE: I thought you found it awkward.

PEA: Maybe I don't know what awkward means.

ROE: Oh, awkward means clumsy, not graceful.

PEA: Oh, I meant to say strikingly wonderful.

ROE: Oh, awkward doesn't mean that.

PEA: Oh, well. I must apologize then. The man is very well made.

ROE: Oh, you don't need to apologize. He doesn't mind your saying he's awkward.

PEA: He is very nice then. He must be a very nice man.

ROE: He's not a man.

PEA: I thought you said he was.

ROE: He is a snowman. That is, he is an imitation of a man. It is snow that has been packed to look like a man.

PEA: What am I made of?

ROE: You're made of flesh. Human flesh.

PEA: And you?

ROE: Human flesh.

PEA (*Pointing to the paper*): And her?

ROE: She's made of human flesh.

PEA (*Pointing*): I look more like him than like her.

ROE (*Looks closely at the picture*): Maybe. (*Short pause*) But he, when it gets warmer, will melt. She will not. And you will not.

PEA: Could I meet her?

ROE: You want to meet her?

PEA: Yes.

ROE (*Reads the caption*):   Her name is Jane Spivak.

PEA: She's beautiful. I would like to look at her. In the flesh.

ROE: I don't know if I could introduce you to her. I don't know
where she lives. But I know other girls I could introduce you
to.

PEA: I don't think I want to meet anyone else. Other girls may
be beautiful, but she looks so very lovely. I like looking at her.
(*Touching the paper*) Even here on this paper. (*Pauses*) We should
be leaving now, Roe, before it gets cold.

ROE: We should wait for Stephen. He said he would meet us
here.

PEA: He did?

ROE: Yes.

PEA: At what time did he say he will come?

ROE: At six.

> (STEPHEN *enters*)

Here he is. (*Reaches for his cane*) We can leave now.

PEA: He may want to stay awhile and warm up.

ROE: Oh, yes, he may.

> (STEPHEN *looks like* PEA *and* ROE. *He wears a brown hat, a
> small checkered jacket, and brown pants. He waddles toward the
> table. The lights fade*)

S C E N E 2

A few minutes later. PEA's head leans on the table. He sleeps. ROE sits on the left. STEPHEN stands upstage of the table.

STEPHEN (*Referring to* PEA):   He is very kind and he could not do harm to anyone.

ROE: Yes. And I don't want any harm to come to him either because he's good.

(*The lights fade*)

S C E N E 3

A month later. PEA sits in the same seat. ROE stands to his left. PEA's necktie is pulled loose. His shirt collar is open and his hat is pushed back as someone who has not slept well. He is somewhat frenetic.

PEA: She is a mystery to me. I look at her as one looks at an animal, loving those eyes, the look in them, the breath as it goes into her shirt, her lips as they close and then part, her mind, the way her body moves. I love her. She is close to my heart the way only an animal can be. And as unfathomable. Looking into her eyes is so quiet—like sleep, like a bed. And she, she is wild like a tiger. She smells like a lion, and she claws like a lion, and yet, in her eyes, she is quiet like a fish.

ROE: That is beautiful, Pea, the way you talk about her.

PEA (*Short of air and making a sound like snoring*):   I am not a person. I am a bat. Look at my skin, see? It is too smooth and too dark. Touch it. This is not like human skin. Look at my nails.

Press them. (ROE *presses* PEA*'s fingers*) See how they turn white?
That's not human. (*Stands and turns his buttocks in* ROE*'s direction*)
Look at that. My anus is violet. Put your finger on it. It is
rough. (*Sits*) When I met her I asked her if it felt as good to
touch her as it felt to look at her. She said, "Try it." (*Moves his
head up and from side to side rapturously*) Do you know what it is
to need someone? The feeling is much deeper than words can
ever say. Do you know what despair is? Anguish? What is it
that makes someone a link between you and your own life? I
hold her close to me and she pushes me away. She finds me
repulsive. She pushed me away and she said, "You rub against
me like a piece of meat. You are a piece of meat. That's what
you are. Like meat at the meat market. You have no brains or
a soul. You are just a piece of meat. Don't rub against me anymore."

ROE (*Putting his hand on* PEA*'s forehead*):   Let me touch you. You
are cold. What a terrible thing to see a young man like you
destroyed like this. Suffering like this.

PEA (*Gets the folded newspaper from inside his jacket*):   I thought if I
kept her picture next to me I'd find relief. But I don't find
relief. There is no relief in this. (*Puts his head on the table*) Is this
why we have come to life? To love like this? And hurt like this?

(*A moment passes.* ROE *puts his hand on* PEA*'s back.* STEPHEN
enters and waddles to the table. He looks at ROE)

ROE: He's drowning. He hurts too much.

(*Lights fade to black*)

The Skit

Dinner was over. The cook was ordered to clear the table as quietly as possible and not to make a noise either with the dishes or her feet. The children were sent to play outside. Osip Fyodorych Klochkov, the host, a gaunt, consumptive man with sunken eyes and a sharp nose, pulled a manuscript out of his pocket and, clearing his throat in embarrassment, began to read a skit of his own composition.

The plot of his short skit was simple and there was nothing in it to offend the censor. Here it is. A government clerk by the name of Yasnosertsev runs onto the stage and announces to his wife that they are about to receive a visit from the ranking official in his department, no less a person than Councilor of State Kleshchov, who had taken a fancy to their daughter Liza. Follows a long monologue by Yasnosertsev on the pleasures of being the father-in-law of a general! "He's simply covered with stars . . . and there's red piping on his trousers, and you sit next to him and—nobody minds! As if you're really not the smallest cog in the whirligig of the universe!" Dreaming thus, the future father-in-law suddenly notices that there is a strong smell of fried goose in the flat. It is awkward to receive an important guest if there is an unpleasant odor in the rooms, and Yasnosertsev starts to bawl his wife out. The wife, exclaiming, "There's no pleasing you!"

begins to howl. The future father-in-law tears his hair and commands his wife to stop crying, for superiors are not received with red eyes. "You fool, go wash your face, you brainless mummy." The wife goes into hysterics. The daughter declares that she cannot live with such quarrelsome parents, and gets dressed to leave the house. Things go from bad to worse. It ends with the important guest finding on the stage a doctor who is applying Garland's extract to the bruises on the husband's forehead, and a police officer, who is drawing up a report on the breach of the peace. That's all. The author also manages to bring on the scene Liza's fiancé, Gransky, a law school graduate, an "advanced" character, who talks about principles, and in the skit seems to exemplify the principle of virtue.

As Klochkov read, he kept glancing at the company out of the corner of his eye to see if they were laughing. To his satisfaction, the guests now and then crammed their fists into their mouths and exchanged looks.

"Well? What do you say?" Klochkov, having finished reading, appealed to his public. "How is it?"

In reply Mitrofan Nikolayevich Zamazurin, the eldest guest, with a fringe of white hair on a scalp as bald as the moon, rose and embraced Klochkov with tears in his eyes.

"Thank you, old man," he said. "That was a treat. You've described it all so well that you even brought tears to my eyes. . . . Let me embrace you once more."

"Excellent! Remarkable!" exclaimed Polumrakov, jumping up. "A genius, a real genius! You know what, brother? Resign from the service and take up writing! Write, write! It's wicked to hide your light under a bushel."

There were congratulations, transports, embraces. . . . They sent for Russian champagne.

Klochkov turned crimson, lost his bearings, and in his excitement began to ambulate about the table.

"I have felt this talent working in me for a long time!" he said, coughing, and waving his arms. "Almost from childhood. . . . I write decently, I'm not without wit. . . . I know the stage—I've taken part in amateur theatricals for the past ten years. . . . What more do I need? If I do a little work in this field, learn certain things—in what way am I inferior to others?"

"Learn certain things, indeed!" said Zamazurin. "There you're right. . . . Only here's what I'd say, old man. You must excuse me, but I stand for the truth. The truth above all else. You bring in Kleshchov, Councilor of State. . . . That's not right, my dear fellow. Essentially, it's nothing, and yet it's awkward, somehow, you know. You take a general, and you—errh . . . Give it up, brother. Our own chief may get angry, he may imagine that you have him in mind. The old man may take offense. And so far he's been very decent to us. Chuck it!"

"That's true." Klochkov grew troubled. "I'll have to make a change. . . . I'll substitute 'your Honor' for 'your Excellency' everywhere. Or else I'll just have no rank—simply: Kleshchov."

"And here's another thing," Polumrakov observed. "Of course, it's a trifle, but it, too, is out of the way . . . it hits you in the face. . . . You have Gransky, the fiancé, tell Liza that if her parents oppose their union, he'll marry her anyway. Perhaps this is a small matter . . . perhaps parents really are sometimes brutes, the way they tyrannize over their children, but nowadays, how shall I put it? I'm afraid you'll get it in the neck!"

"Yes, it's a bit strong," Zamazurin agreed. "You ought to smooth over that passage somehow. . . . And you should cut out that speech about how pleasant it is to be your superior's father-in-law. Yes, it *is* pleasant, but you poke fun at it. It's no laughing matter, brother. Our chief, too, married a girl without money; does it mean that he did something wrong? Is that your opinion? Wouldn't it offend him? Well, suppose he goes to the theater and sees this skit of yours . . . will he like it? And remember, he backed you when both you and Salaleyev applied for a subsidy! 'He's a sick man,' he said, 'he needs money more than Salaleyev does.' Don't you see?"

"You were taking him off, weren't you? Admit it," Bulyagin said, winking at the author.

"Not at all!" protested Klochkov. "I wasn't thinking of anybody in particular, I swear!"

"Come, come—you can't fool us! We all know he chases after skirts. You've caught *that*. But you know what? Cut out that police officer. Better do without him. . . . And you don't want this Gransky, either. A hero, God knows what department he's in, and he talks so queerly. . . . It would be all right if you condemned him, but, on the contrary, you cotton to him. Maybe he is a decent sort, but the devil himself couldn't figure him out! You can imagine almost anything about him. . . ."

"And do you know who that Yasnosertsev is? It's the Yenakin in our office. Klochkov certainly had him in mind. A titular councilor, he and his wife are always fighting, there's a daughter, too. . . . That's him to the life. Thanks, friend! Serves the blackguard right! You've taken him down a peg!"

"True enough, but there's something else to be said about Yenakin," Zamazurin said, with a sigh. "A bad egg, a rascal, still, he always invites you to his house, he's godfather to your Nastya. . . . It's not right, Osip! Leave him out of it! It's my opinion you ought to give up this kind of business, by God. Before you know it there'll be talk: who, how, why? You'll only regret it!"

"That's so," Polumrakov chimed in. "It's tomfoolery, but this tomfoolery may cause trouble that it will take ten years to set right. It's a mistake to start all this, Osip. You're not the one to try to be a Gogol or a Krylov. They were, really, men of learning; but what education did you get? You're a worm, you're too small to be seen! A fly can crush you. Give it up, brother! If our chief finds out, then . . . Chuck it!"

"Tear it up!" whispered Bulyagin. "We won't tell anybody. If they ask us, we'll say that you read something to us, but that we didn't understand it."

"Why say anything? There's no need to talk," declared Zamazurin. "If they ask us, well, then . . . we're not going to lie. A man thinks of himself first. . . . That's how it is: you people do all kinds of mischief, and others have to pay for it! I get the worst of it. You're a sick man, no one will call you to account, but we won't be spared. I don't like it, by God!"

"Quiet, gentlemen! Someone's coming. . . . Put it away, Klochkov."

Klochkov, turning pale, quickly hid his manuscript, scratched the back of his head, and grew thoughtful.

"It's true," he sighed. "There'll be talk . . . all kinds of guesses. . . . Maybe there's something in my skit that we don't see but others will find there. . . . I'll tear it up. And you, friends, please . . . don't say anything to anybody."

The Russian champagne was brought in. The guests drank it, and dispersed.

A Dopey Fairy Tale

by

MICHAEL WELLER

CHARACTERS

SMILE

FATHER BAKER

MOTHER BAKER

CLARENCE

CHATTER (the dog)

MAYOR

MAGISTRATE

MINISTER

FEMALE FROG

MALE FROG

SAD PRINCESS GLADYS

This should all be played real dopey.

> *Enter* SMILE, *the narrator, in a swallowtail coat and top hat, and an enormous fixed smile that never leaves his face.*

SMILE: Once upon a very long time ago, in a far distant fairy-tale kingdom in the tiny village of, oh, say, Placeville, there lived a family of jolly bakers.

> (*Lights up on family group:* FATHER, MOTHER, CLARENCE, *and* CHATTER, *a dog*)

SMILE: There was the jolly father, Mr. Baker . . .

FATHER: Pie, bread, cookies, cake,
These are the things I like to bake.

SMILE: His jolly, good-hearted, but somewhat impractical wife, Mrs. Baker . . .

MOTHER: The Smiths ordered two loaves of pumpernickel bread, but I threw in a dozen chocolate chip cookies for free because they love them so much and even though we may end up losing money, still, just think how happy the Smiths will be.

FATHER: You're so impractical, dear.

MOTHER: But I'm very good-hearted.

SMILE: Then there was Chatter the dog, who could do something most dogs can't.

CHATTER (*Digging*):   I could have sworn I buried that bone right here in the front yard . . . !

SMILE: He could talk!

CHATTER: Or was it the backyard? Or under the willow by the river?

SMILE: But he had a terrible terrible memory.

CHATTER (*To* SMILE):   I can talk, can't I? Give a dog a break.

SMILE: And last, but most important of all, was their son Clarence, who until recently had been a very ordinary little boy, until he discovered that he had a very extraordinary talent.

CLARENCE (*Imitating* SMILE):   "Once upon a very long time ago, in the tiny village of, oh, say, Placeville . . ."

SMILE: He could imitate anyone he met . . . perfectly.

CLARENCE: "Perfectly."

SMILE: Isn't that adorable?

FATHER: You be careful who you make fun of, boy. Not everyone likes to see themselves in a comical light.

CLARENCE: I don't mean any harm, Father, sir. I just enjoy seeing people laugh. . . .

SMILE: Every year, the ruler of the kingdom, the orphaned regent Sad Princess Gladys, would wander from the royal palace for one entire month.

(PRINCESS GLADYS *crosses stage singing the first phrase of* "*Stormy Weather*")

Where she went no one knew, but when she returned, she held a royal feast and each village in the kingdom sent to her table the one dish they made best. For one's village to send one's dish was a great, great honor.

FATHER: Mother, Clarence, Chatter, guess who's coming to pay us a visit tomorrow? The Mayor, the Minister, and the Magistrate.

MOTHER: The Three Big M's of Placeville? But, dear, they would only visit us at this time of year if . . .

FATHER: That's right! They have agreed to sample our pastries and consider them for the official entry of Placeville at the royal feast of Sad Princess Gladys. If chosen, we'll be summoned to the palace in a royal coach, the Princess will allow us to grovel at her feet, word will spread, our pastry will become famous throughout the land, we'll open a chain of stores . . . McBaker's! Invest in real estate. Diversify. We'll be rich, rich, rich!

CHATTER: I'm so excited I could bark, if I remembered how!

(FAMILY *sets up table of pastries*)

SMILE: So all that night the Bakers baked in preparation for their important visitors, and while the town slept peacefully, the dark air filled with savory odors from the Bakers' chimney: jam tarts and quince tarts and rhubarb pie and veal pie and chocolate chip cookies and oatmeal raisin cookies and blueberry muffins and egg bread and sesame rolls and strawberry flans and cinnamon doughnuts and honey popovers and cannoli. No, wait, not cannoli. I'm getting carried away. I just happen to love cannoli. Have you ever tasted it with espresso cof— (*Stops*) Never mind. The next morning, when all was ready, Father Baker called his family together.

FATHER: Now, Clarence, remember, we must do everything in

our power to please the Three Big M's of Placeville, so be po-
lite at all times, speak only when spoken to, and, above all,
none of your infernal imitations. The punch, Mother . . .
explain.

MOTHER: There are two bowls of punch. The one at this end of
the table has in it a little something to make our honored guests
feel pleasant and look kindly upon our baked goods. The one
at this end is plain old punch. Children and dogs drink from
this one. The rest of us from the other.

CLARENCE: Yes, Mother.

MOTHER: Chatter?

CHATTER: Under the shed! That's where I buried it. What? Oh,
yes, I understand.

SMILE: And with that, the guests arrived.

(*Enter* MAYOR, MINISTER, *and* MAGISTRATE, *all very self-
important*)

FATHER: Mr. Mayor, Mr. Minister, Mr. Magistrate, what an
honor to have you with us today. Please, help yourselves.

MAYOR (*With flourishes*):   And what a delectable array of the baker's art you have endeavored to present before us on this hal-
lowed day of sampling and decision. The smell alone arouses
within my person elements of compliment which I would hasten to utter if time and circumstances were of a more flexible
aspect, but that being not the case, let us eschew becoming
lost in the byways of preamble, and to the tasting!

MOTHER: Chatter, some punch for the guests.

(CHATTER *obeys, putting punch in cups and passing them out*)

FATHER: And how do you enjoy the pineapple upside-down
cake, Mr. Minister?

MINISTER: F-f-f-f-first rate, I m-m-m-must say.

MOTHER: Mr. Magistrate, those are the chocolate éclairs, one of our specialties.

MAGISTRATE: Are they not topped with chocolate? This is visible. Have they not the oblong shape of éclairs? This is patent. So, altogether, are they not chocolate éclairs? Of this I'm aware.

CHATTER (*With two cups*): This one's for you, Clarence, and this one's for the Mayor. No, wait. This one . . . right paw, left paw. Which paw do you eat your soup with? Oh! I remember now. *This* one's yours.

CLARENCE (*Drinking*): Aren't they silly, Chatter. I bet if they could see themselves, they'd howl with laughter.

CHATTER: Remember what your father said, Clarence.

CLARENCE: I know, I know.

CHATTER: What *did* he say? There was something you shouldn't do. Or was it *should*?

MAYOR: Mr. and Mrs. Baker, may I just say that even having concluded a mere fraction of the available sampling here before us, I find myself vigorously propelled towards a favorable reception vis-à-vis the fruits of your artistry, if I may put it that way.

MAGISTRATE: Is the flavor not superior? This has been experienced. Might our town take pride in such an entry? This is possible.

MINISTER: D-d-d-d-d-d-d-d-d-d-dee-li-li-li-li-licious.

FATHER: Well, Mother, what do you say to that?

MOTHER (*After a pause*): Have seconds!

(ALL *laugh politely*)

FATHER: Clarence, would you like to thank our guests?

CLARENCE (*Looking woozy*):   Th-th-th-th-thank you o-o-o-one and
all.

MINISTER (*Pleased*):   It's n-n-n-nothing, my b-b-b-. What did he
just s-s-s-s-say?

MOTHER: Clarence!

CHATTER (*To himself*):   Left paw, right paw. Uh-oh.

MAGISTRATE: Was your son not mocking the Minister? This is
suggested.

CLARENCE: And is the suggestion not amusing? It is. Are we not
on the verge of laughter? We should be.

FATHER: Not another word, Clarence. Go directly to your
room.

MAYOR: Am I receiving the impression that your son's behavioral peculiarity contains within it elements of imitation which
could be taken to reflect upon certain members of the company
present in the area of this room today?

CLARENCE: The behavioral aspects in question contain within
their limits only a desire to illustrate to the collected population within the purviews of the area under our roof a certain
humorous impression . . .

MINISTER: He's making f-f-f-f-fun of us.

CLARENCE: You're making f-f-f-fun of yourself.

MAGISTRATE: Is my temper not rising at this display? This is
tangible. Am I not about to explode with anger? This is im-
minent.

CLARENCE: Do you not always answer your own questions?
This we've observed.

FATHER: To your room!

CLARENCE: Is anyone interested in what you have to say? This is doubtful.

MAYOR: How dare you! Take that! (*Hits* CLARENCE) And that. (*Hits him again*) And that and that and that.

(THE THREE BIG M's *pounce on* CLARENCE *and beat him*)

MOTHER: Stop, you bullies, he's only a little boy!

FATHER: Perhaps now he'll know better than to disobey his father!

MOTHER: Chatter, do something to frighten them off. Bark. Growl. Be menacing.

CHATTER (*Pronouncing the words*): Arf. Arf. Grrr. Grrr. Bark. Rolf. Woof-woof. Something's lacking.

(*The beating stops*)

MAYOR: Needless to articulate, no elements of the baker's trade will represent this village at the royal feast, this year or ever!

MINISTER: P-p-p-p-astries be damned.

MAGISTRATE: Are we not leaving in a huff? We are!

(THE THREE BIG M's *exit in a huff*)

MOTHER: Oh, Clarence, darling, are you all right?

CLARENCE: Why did they do that, Mother? I thought they'd find it funny.

FATHER: They're laughing, all right. And guess who's the joke? No meeting with Sad Princess Gladys. No McBaker's. All our dreams in ruins. Tomorrow you will come with me and apologize to the Three Big Ms of Placeville. We will humble ourselves before them and beg to have our pastry reconsidered!

CLARENCE: How can I apologize when I did nothing wrong?

FATHER: Are you contradicting me, young man?

MOTHER: Don't be so hard on him, dear. He only meant to amuse.

FATHER: I'm locking you in your room until you agree to come with me and apologize. No back talk. Go to your room.

SMILE: And so, that night, Clarence was locked up alone in his room, while Chatter sat outside the door listening to his beloved friend's sighs. Oh, dear, this part's so sad, I can barely bring myself to watch.

(CHATTER *and* CLARENCE *on opposite sides of make-believe door*)

CHATTER: How ya doin', Clar?

CLARENCE: Sigh.

CHATTER: Oh, boy. My screw-up. There I was, one of each punch in separate cups, and then I remembered . . . it's under the bench in the town square, that's where I buried my bone. And everything else went clean out of my head. (*Pauses*) Clar, talk to me. (*Pauses*) God, when you did the Mayor I was so near laughing out loud I nearly had to run and find a tree to pee on. Do him again, I really get a kick out of that one. Clar?

CLARENCE (*After a pause, trying*):   I . . . I can't.

CHATTER: Why not?

CLARENCE: Nothing comes out.

CHATTER: The Magistrate, he's easy, I can almost handle that one myself.

CLARENCE (*After a pause*):   It's no use, Chatter. I try and try, but all I remember is their angry faces and how they beat me, and nothing comes out.

CHATTER: Bad attitude, Clar.

CLARENCE: Well, what else am I to think?

CHATTER: Try this on for size. "Where there's life, there's hope." And how about "Every cloud has a silver lining." (*Pauses*) Darn, there's another one . . . it's right on the tip of my tongue. "Go for it," that's the one.

CLARENCE: Go for what?

CHATTER: Your talent. We'll venture forth to search for where it went, and we'll have some adventures, and then we'll find it and we can all live happily ever after.

CLARENCE: You're right, Chatter! Why didn't I think of that? But first I have to escape from my room.

CHATTER: Leave that part to me.

SMILE: And so Chatter, using skills he'd acquired here and there, picked the lock on Clarence's bedroom door, and that night two figures could be seen slipping across the shadows of the village square, out past the fields of the surrounding farms, across the river and into the dark dark forest beyond. After what seemed like hours, it dawned on them that they were lost.

CLARENCE: Chatter, where are we?

CHATTER: Well, I'm over here and you're over there. After that it's anyone's guess.

SMILE: Now comes the scary bit. I love to be frightened. Like when someone sneaks up behind you and goes "Boo!" Isn't that great? Anyway, all around them, the frightened pair heard strange noises from the depths of the dark dark forest.

(*Strange animal noises*)

CLARENCE: Boy, Chatter, there's sure some spooky noises in the forest.

CHATTER: That's not the only spooky thing, Clar. Look up ahead!

CLARENCE: What is it?

CHATTER: Whatever it is, there's two of them. A pair of spooky things.

(*Enter* TWO FROGS, *a* MALE—M.F.—*and a* FEMALE—F.F.—*hopping*)

BOTH FROGS: Ribbit-ribbit. Ribbit-ribbit.

CLARENCE: They sound like frogs.

CHATTER: They sound like *big* frogs.

CLARENCE: Try talking to them.

CHATTER: Clarence, frogs don't talk.

CLARENCE: Neither do dogs.

CHATTER: Good point, good point. Hey, you two. You two frogs! What's the deal here?

F.F.:   We are enchanted frogs.

CHATTER: Enchanted frogs, God, what an image.

F.F.:   You're here because you think you've lost your talent, Clarence. But it isn't true. All you have lost is the courage to use it. You must find your courage, and once you've found it, you must never again let it go, no matter how angry it may make people.

CLARENCE: But where shall I look?

F.F.:   We're coming to that, take it easy.

M.F.:   You start, dear.

F.F.:   Only one person in the kingdom can help you, Clarence, and that is the orphaned regent Sad Princess Gladys. Seek her out, discover what makes her sad, then find a way to bring a smile to her face, for it is written that he who makes the princess smile shall one day be king.

M.F.:   And being a king is a very big deal. If that doesn't restore your courage, forget it.

CLARENCE: But this is the month the princess disappears, to whence no one knows. How shall I ever find her?

F.F.:   You must undergo the following trial. Do exactly as we say and no harm shall come to you. But one mistake and, poof, you'll both be turned to Dacron.

M.F.:   Rock, darling. They'll be turned to rock.

F.F.:   Whatever. First, you must walk straight ahead in the direction we point, and for three days and three nights you may not stop, nor may you look to the right or to the left.

M.F.:   On the third day . . .

F.F.:   And no food. You can't eat anything.

M.F.:   That's right. Then, on day three, a great rain will fall, and before a single droplet can touch you, you must say the words "Gladys, where art thou and what makes thee so sad?" Whereupon you will become tiny enough to walk between the raindrops, and this is very important . . .

F.F.:   . . . because if you are wet when you reach the Mighty Oak of Oaks, you will be turned instantly into mohair.

M.F.:   Rock, dear.

F.F.:   You tell it your way, I'll tell it mine. Have you both understood?

CLARENCE: Are you getting all this, Chatter?

CHATTER: You lost me at the raindrops.

M.F.:   At the Mighty Oak of Oaks, you will find lying nearby a stick in the shape of a Y. This you must beat against the tree. The rain will stop instantly, a bolt of lightning will strike the oak and render it in twain . . .

CLARENCE: Is all this really necessary? It sounds awfully complicated.

F.F.:   You want to know if there's a shortcut, sonny? Of course there's a shortcut, there's always a shortcut.

CLARENCE: Perhaps you could tell us what it is.

M.F.:   If we had wanted to do that, we'd have told you in the first place. We're enchanted frogs. We call the shots.

F.F.:   You want to do it your way, go ahead, see what happens, but don't expect any help from us. And remember, one wrong move, hello mohair.

M.F.:   Ribbit-ribbit.

(BOTH FROGS *exit*)

CLARENCE: No, wait . . .

SMILE: As the enchanted frogs leapt away, Clarence realized with growing horror what a desperate situation they were in.

CLARENCE: Oh, Chatter, now what do we do? One wrong move and we'll be fabric.

CHATTER: Let me think. I've been in this situation before.

CLARENCE: You have?

CHATTER: Oh, you know, other fairy tales. The faithful companion, that sort of thing.

CLARENCE: You've been in other fairy tales?

CHATTER: Did you think I was a one-tale dog? The thing is, there was always a way out.

SMILE: Whereupon Chatter, barely knowing why, but overwhelmed with a certainty that he was very close to the bone, set to digging with a frenzy.

(CHATTER *digs with a fury*)

CHATTER: Oh, yes, that smell, that smell. A nice, juicy tibia. And with bits of meat still clinging to the ends, if memory serves. (*Finds something*) I've got something. This isn't a bone.

CLARENCE: It's a diamond, Chatter. It's the largest diamond I ever saw.

CHATTER: Just my luck. Go for a meal, end up with a rock.

CLARENCE: Listen, it's starting to hum.

CHATTER: Great. A humming diamond, just what I need. Next thing you know, it'll probably talk.

VOICE: Who are you two, and what brings you here?

CHATTER: What did I tell you!

CLARENCE: No, Chatter, look over there . . . !

SMILE: As they turned, they beheld the most beautiful creature they had ever seen. Her lips were like pearls. Rubies, sorry, rubies. Her skin was like pearls. Or alabaster. Also, she looked very sad.

PRINCESS: How did you know where to find the diamond from my missing father's crown?

CLARENCE: We are looking for the orphaned regent, Sad Princess Gladys.

PRINCESS: Look no more.

CHATTER: You don't understand, lady, we have important business with the woman.

PRINCESS: I am she who you seek.

CLARENCE: But you . . . you're . . . beautiful.

PRINCESS: I know. Beautiful . . . and sad.

CHATTER (*After a pause*): Is that it? Have we done it?

CLARENCE: First we must learn why she's sad, then I must make her smile.

CHATTER: Why?

CLARENCE: To get back my courage.

CHATTER: Oh, right, right. You go ahead, I'll cover you from behind. Wait, that's a different fairy tale. Or was it a western?

CLARENCE: Princess Gladys . . .

CHATTER: Clar, was I in a western?

CLARENCE: Princess Gladys, I've been seeking you to ask a question. What makes you so sad? Will you answer?

PRINCESS: Since you discovered where I buried the largest diamond from my missing father's crown . . . yes. I will tell you what I've told no living creature before this day. I am in mourning for my life. No, that's wrong. I am a seagull. No, that's not it.

CHATTER: She's a real hoot, this one.

PRINCESS: I am forever sad because my mother and father, who others knew as the king and queen because that is what they were, disappeared when I was first born, spirited away by a witch, they say, and by a magic spell turned into creatures of another species. Each year I take a month off to look for them in the woods, petting all the animals I find, hoping thereby to recognize, by a touch or a gesture, some sign of my heritage. Each year I fail, alas, and then I return to the palace and hold a feast to help take my mind off it. Eating sometimes helps. It's a form of substitute behavior common among the well-to-do, and I'm no exception.

CLARENCE: If you were a mere baby when they disappeared, isn't it time to stop being sad?

PRINCESS: But I don't wish to stop. And even if I wished to, it would be wrong, terribly wrong. You see, it's good to be sad. I want everyone in my kingdom to be sad in every part of their body, just as I am. My skin is sad, my hands are sad, my hair is by . . . no, that's not it. My eyes are sad, my lips are sad, and I could cry until I melt into a warm puddle of salt tears.

(CLARENCE, *without realizing it, starts to imitate her*)

CLARENCE: And then my tears will mix with the soil and water all the land until trees grow sad and the grass grows sad and the rivers run sadly through the kingdom . . .

PRINCESS: Are you making fun of me, commoner?

CLARENCE: And even then I won't be satisfied until the clouds breathe in my tears from the forest and cause the rain to fall sad and the wind to blow sad and the entire world to weep and weep and weep.

PRINCESS: I am a princess. Keep it up and I'll make a lot of trouble for you.

CLARENCE: I'm your subject. Keep it up and you'll make a lot of trouble for me.

(CLARENCE *is now enjoying it*)

PRINCESS: One more word and I shall strike you with my royal open palm.

CLARENCE: But sadly, princess, do it sadly.

(PRINCESS *raises her hand to strike. Stops*)

PRINCESS: Is that really the way I look?

CHATTER: He's got you down to a tee, lady.

PRINCESS (*Smiles, then laughs*):   That's ridiculous. You mean I've been going around all these years looking like that? Why didn't someone tell me? (*Laughs*) I could die with shame if it wasn't so funny.

CHATTER: Hey, Clar, do you realize what you just did? You imitated her. And she's laughing!

CLARENCE: It just came out. She looked in my eyes, and I don't know . . . it gave me courage. Is that what love is?

(*Enter* FROGS)

F.F.:   Look, dear, she's laughing.

M.F.:   If she laughs, the spell is broken. We forgot to say that part.

(BOTH FROGS *stand up straight*, now the KING *and* QUEEN)

QUEEN: Darling!

KING: My dear daughter.

PRINCESS: Mother? Father? It's really you. And guess what, I'm in love. With him. What's your name?

CLARENCE: Clarence.

PRINCESS: Can I marry him, please, please, please?

QUEEN: Sure.

PRINCESS: Thanks.

KING: Welcome, Clarence, to the royal family, ribbit-rib . . . whoops.

SMILE: And with that, Clarence returned home a hero, and Placeville welcomed him with open arms.

(*Enter* FATHER, MOTHER, MAYOR, MAGISTRATE, *and* MINISTER)

MOTHER: My son, the king!

FATHER: Good boy, good good boy.

MAYOR: We're pleased and anxious to suck up to certain elements of the newly returned royal personage.

MINISTER: His ass-ass-ass-ass-astonishing talent, in particul-l-l-l-lar.

MAGISTRATE: A question? An answer!

SMILE: So Mr. Baker got his franchise, Clarence regained his talent forever, and year after year the palace rang with laughter as he imitated everyone in sight. And at long long last, Chatter found his bone.

(SMILE *removes bone from inside pocket, or produces it like magic.* CHATTER, *behind him, approaches the bone, but the moment before he clamps his jaw around it,* SMILE *remembers something and begins to speak, waving the bone oblivious of* CHATTER, *who stands right behind him, trying to grab it with his mouth*)

The moral?

ALL: The moral.

SMILE: If you have a talent, don't be frightened when it upsets people . . . because one day you'll marry a princess and no one will dare mess with you! Not very universal, is it? I'm terrible at ends. How about . . . let's see . . . pompous behavior deserves to be laughed at? Or . . . don't pooh-pooh large frogs in the forest, they may be royalty. Or this: Anton Chekhov was a great writer, but when you quote him out of context even his dialogue sounds laughable. Or . . .

CHATTER: Give a dog a break.

(SMILE *hands him the bone*)

SMILE: And they all lived happily ever after.

CLARENCE (*Like* SMILE):   Because I commanded it, and I was the king.

SMILE: The end.

(ALL *bow and exit*)

The Eve of the Trial

The Defendant's Story

S ure to be trouble, sir!" said the coachman, turning towards me, and pointing with his whip at a hare running across our road.

I had no need of a hare to tell me that my future was desperate. I was driving to the district assizes at X———, where I had to appear in the dock for bigamy. The weather was terrible. When, towards nightfall, I arrived at the post station, I was so chilled, soaked, and stupefied by the monotonous jolting of the road that I looked like a man who had been covered with snow, drenched with water, and badly whacked. I was met at the station by the station superintendent, a tall man in blue-striped underpants, bald, sleepy, and with a mustache which seemed to grow out of his nostrils and looked as if it would prevent him from smelling anything.

And it must be admitted that there was plenty to smell. When the supervisor, muttering something, breathing heavily through his nose and scratching his neck, opened the door of the station "rest room" and silently showed me my place of rest with his elbow, I was overwhelmed—almost to suffocation—by a strong smell of something sour, sealing wax, and squashed bugs. The unpainted wooden walls were illuminated by a small tin lamp which stood on the table and was smoking like matchwood.

"Your place certainly stinks, signor!" I said, going in and putting my suitcase on the table.

The supervisor sniffed the air and shook his head incredulously.

"Smells as it always does," he said, and scratched himself. "That's just your impression, coming from outside. The coachmen sleep with their horses, and the gentlemen don't smell."

I dismissed the supervisor, and began inspecting my temporary abode. The sofa on which I would have to recline was as wide as a double bed, covered with oilcloth, and as cold as ice. Apart from the sofa, the room contained a large iron stove, the table with the above-mentioned lamp, someone's felt boots, someone's traveling handbag, and a screen which barricaded one corner of the room. Behind the screen someone was peacefully sleeping. When I had made my inspection I made the sofa ready for the night and began to undress. My nose soon became accustomed to the stench. I took off my frock coat, trousers, and boots, stretched and scratched to my heart's content, smiled, hugged myself, and began to skip around the iron stove, raising high my bare feet. . . . This skipping warmed me up even more. After that it only remained to lie down on the sofa and go to sleep, but at that moment something odd happened. By chance my glance fell on the screen and . . . imagine my horror! A woman's head, with loose hair, black eyes, and teeth bared, was looking at me from behind the screen. Her black eyebrows were twitching, pretty little dimples were playing on her cheeks—so she must have been laughing. I was embarrassed. The head, noticing that I had seen it, also became embarrassed, and hid. With eyes cast down and a guilty look, I went meekly to the sofa, lay down, and covered myself with my fur coat.

What a business! I thought. That means she saw me skipping! That's too bad. . . .

And, as I recalled the features of that pretty little face, I fell to dreaming. Pictures, each more beautiful and seductive than the last, thronged in my imagination and . . . and, as if to punish me for sinful thoughts, a sharp pain suddenly burned my right cheek. I clutched at it, caught nothing, but guessed what had happened: there was a smell of squashed bug.

At the same moment I heard a woman's voice. "It really is the very devil! These damned bugs obviously want to eat me up!"

Mm! . . . I remembered my good habit of always taking insect powder with me when I traveled. And I had not changed my habit this time. I took the tin of powder out of my suitcase in a matter of seconds. It only remained to offer the pretty head a remedy for bugs and—friendship would be struck up. But how could I offer it?

"This is awful!"

"Madam," I said in my most honeyed tones. "If I understand your last exclamation rightly, you are being bitten by bugs. Now, I have some insect powder. If you wish, then . . ."

"Oh yes, please!"

"In that case," I said, delighted, "I'll just . . . put on my fur coat and bring it to you. . . ."

"No, no . . . give it me through the screen, but don't come here!"

"Of course I meant through the screen. Don't be afraid: I'm not a bashi-bazouk. . . ."

"Who knows? You're just a passerby, after all. . . ."

"Mm. . . . And even if I was to go behind the screen . . . there wouldn't be much harm in it . . . all the more so as I'm a doctor," I lied. "Doctors, policemen, and ladies' hairdressers have the right to intrude in people's private lives."

"Is it true that you're a doctor? Seriously?"

"Word of honor. So may I bring you the insect powder?"

"Well, if you're a doctor, I suppose. . . . But why should you have the trouble? I can send my husband to you. . . . Fedya!" said the brunette, dropping her voice. "Fedya! Wake up, you mutt! Get up and go around the screen! The doctor's so kind, he's offering us some insect powder."

The presence of "Fedya" behind the screen was shattering

news to me. I was thunderstruck. . . . My heart was filled with the feeling which, in all probability, rifle-cocks feel after a misfire: shame, vexation, and sorrow. . . . I felt so upset about it and, when he appeared from behind the screen, I felt that Fedya must be such a scoundrel that I almost shouted for help. Fedya turned out to be a tall, sinewy man of about fifty, with little gray whiskers, the set lips of a civil servant, and with blue veins running untidily over his nose and temples. He was in dressing gown and slippers.

"It's very kind of you, doctor . . ." he said, taking the insect powder from me and turning around to go back behind the screen. "Merci. . . . You were caught by the snowstorm too?"

"Yes!" I snarled, lying down on the sofa and furiously pulling the fur coat over me. "Yes!"

"I see. . . . Zinochka, there's a bug running down your little nose! Allow me to remove it!"

"All right!" laughed Zinochka. "You didn't get it! You're a senior civil servant, everyone's afraid of you, but you can't deal with a bug!"

"Zinochka, in front of strangers . . ." (A sigh.) "You're always . . . Honestly . . ."

"The swine! They won't let me sleep!" I grumbled, getting angry without myself knowing why.

But soon husband and wife fell silent. I closed my eyes and, in order to fall asleep, began to think of nothing at all. But half an hour, an hour passed . . . and I was not asleep. Finally my neighbors, too, began to toss and turn and grumble in whispers.

"It's amazing, even insect powder doesn't do any good!" growled Fedya. "There's so many of them, these bugs! Doctor! Zinochka wants me to ask you why these bugs smell so loathsomely."

We chatted. We talked about bugs, the weather, the Russian winter, medicine—which I know about as much about as I do about astronomy—we talked about Edison. . . .

"Don't be shy, Zinochka. . . . After all, he's a doctor!" I heard a whisper after the conversation about Edison. "Don't stand on ceremony, ask him. . . . There's nothing to be afraid of. Shervetsov didn't do any good, perhaps this one will. . . ."

"Ask yourself!" whispered Zinochka.

"Doctor," said Fedya, addressing himself to me. "Why does my wife get a congestion in her chest sometimes? A cough, you know . . . it feels congested, you know, a sort of clot. . . ."

"That's a long story, it's impossible to say at once . . ." I replied, trying to dodge the question.

"Well, what if it is a long story? We've got plenty of time . . . we aren't sleeping anyway. . . . Have a look at her, old fellow! I should tell you, Shervetsov is treating her. . . . He's a good man, but . . . who can tell? I've no faith in him! No faith at all! I can see you don't want to, but do be so kind! You examine her, and while you're doing it I'll go to the superintendent and order a samovar to be put on."

Fedya shuffled off in his slippers and left the room. I went behind the screen. Zinochka was sitting on a wide sofa, surrounded by a quantity of pillows, and holding up her lace collar.

"Show me your tongue!" I began, sitting down beside her and frowning.

She put out her tongue and laughed. It was an ordinary, red tongue. I tried to feel her pulse.

"Mm! . . ." I mooed, unable to find the pulse.

I cannot remember what other questions I put to her as I looked at her little laughing face—I only remember that by the time I had finished examining her I felt such a silly idiot that I definitely could not cope with any more questions.

It all ended with Fedya, Zinochka, and myself sitting around the samovar; a prescription had to be written, and I composed it according to all the rules of medicine:

        Rp. Sic transit   0.05
        Gloria Mundi   1.0
        Aquae destillatae   0.1

One tablespoonful every two hours.

Mrs. Syelov.

Dr. Zaitsev.

In the morning I was on the point of leaving and, with suitcase in hand, was saying farewell forever to my new friends, when Fedya buttonholed me and, holding a ten-ruble note, tried to make me take it:

"Oh, but it's your duty to take it! I always pay for all honest labor! You've studied and you've worked! You've sweated blood to acquire your knowledge! I understand that!"

There was nothing else to be done, I had to take the ten rubles!

That, in general outline, is how I spent the eve of my trial. I will not describe my feelings when the door opened in front of me and the bailiff showed me into the dock. I will only say that I grew pale and embarrassed when, looking around, I saw thousands of eyes fixed on me; and I felt my last hour had come when I looked at the serious, solemnly important faces of the jury. . . .

But I cannot describe—and you cannot imagine—my horror when, raising my eyes to the table covered with red cloth, I saw in the public prosecutor's place—whom do you think?—Fedya! He was sitting there and writing something. As I looked at him I remembered the bugs, Zinochka, my examination of her—and it was not a mere shiver that ran down my spine, but the whole Arctic Ocean. . . . When he had finished writing, he looked at me. At first he did not recognize me, but then his pupils dilated and his jaw dropped weakly . . . his hands shook. He got up slowly and fixed a glassy stare on me. I too got up, not knowing myself why I did so, and stared at him. . . .

"Will the defendant please tell the court his name and particulars?" the judge began.

The public prosecutor sat down and drank a glass of water. Cold sweat broke out on his forehead.

Well, now I'm in for it! I thought.

Everything pointed to the fact that the public prosecutor

was determined to cook my goose. He kept on losing his temper, went minutely into the witnesses' evidence, was crotchety, grumbled. . . .

However, it's time I finished this. I am writing it in the court-room during the luncheon interval. . . . In a moment the prose-cutor will make his speech.

I wonder what will happen?

Eve of the Trial

by

SAMM-ART WILLIAMS

MA LOLA — *Owns a run-down rural rooming house just outside Baton Rouge, Louisiana.*

LESTER SIMMONS — *The "hanging judge" in charge of the Circuit Court in Baton Rouge. Southern.*

PEARL SIMMONS — *Lester's wife. Southern.*

TATE — *A deputy sheriff from Baton Rouge, who is assigned to take Alex and his two wives to Baton Rouge to stand trial for bigamy.*

ALEX BUSHKIN (ALEXIS BUSKENOV) — *Russian expatriate now stranded in the southern United States as a result of the Bolshevik Revolution, which saw his family give their property to the state. Alex believes that the Bolsheviks are going to assassinate him, so he marries two women and sets out for Utah, where he will live in disguise as a Mormon. Educated, Western manner, pompous. Very charming to the ladies.*

LILLY — *One of Alex's wives. Lilly once worked in the Scarlet Garter, a whorehouse in Charleston, South Carolina. Southern.*

KITTY — *One of Alex's wives. Kitty is a good friend of Lilly's and is also an ex-employee of the Scarlet Garter. Southern.*

Time: August 1919

Place: Ma Lola's rooming house just outside Baton Rouge, Louisiana

Set units: 1. Living room, sparsely furnished, with kerosene lamps
2. Bare stage area

Note: The weather is hot, humid, and sticky. The mosquitoes bite with a vengeance and one's clothing seldom dries from yesterday's sweat. Not to mention that the air seldom moves in this part of Louisiana. Especially at . . . midnight.

>*It is midnight. Lights come up on the interior of* MA LOLA's *rooming house. The furnishings are spare and rustic. The house in general is a filthy mess. As the lights come up, we hear the sound of crickets and the hooting of an owl.* MA LOLA, PEARL, *and* LESTER *enter the living room.* LESTER *is tired and weary.* PEARL *is nursing stomach cramps from an advanced case of diarrhea.* MA *lights a kerosene lamp, stage left. Suddenly* MA *shouts aloud and stomps on a water bug several times.*

MA: Ahhhh! Ahhhh! Little varmints! Damn little varmints!

LESTER: Jesus Christ, Lola, you plumb near give me a heart attack! What is it?!

PEARL: My bowels won't take that kind of shock, Lola. I swear they won't.

MA: There's another one!

LESTER: What?

MA: Water bugs. I got the biggest ones in the state. I swear to you they's crossed between a snappin' turtle and a jackass, 'cause I don't know nothing in tarnation that can stand these number nines of mine, 'cept them bugs. Well, the place is yours. I ain't had time to do much cleaning . . . as usual.

LESTER: As tired as I am I could sleep on a bed of rocks. I been up all night for the past two nights nursing poor Pearl's condition. With a big trial comin' up in the mornin', I gotta get some sleep.

MA: Big trial?

LESTER: Some damn foreigner . . . but it'll all come out in the wash.

MA: I tell you outright, Judge Simmons, it ain't often we get important guests like you and the missus stopping in.

PEARL: Could we get some rest now? I'm feeling powerful sick.

MA (*Whispering to* LESTER): Is the missus in a family way?

LESTER: Which room . . . please?

MA: Is it your time of the month, honey? I got vinegar and . . .

PEARL: A bed, please. I've had diarrhea for two days.

MA: Second room on the left. Straight back. I'll see to your horse and wagon.

(We hear an owl's hoot)

That owl hootin' like he's hoarse. Means either rain . . . or snow.

LESTER: In August?

MA: If it's God's will. If you have to go to the outhouse, there's plenty newspaper and a Sears catalogue already out there. *(Exits)*

PEARL: My Lord, this place is just a bug-infested dump. If this storm wasn't coming up, we could've made Baton Rouge.

LESTER: It was either here or the back of the wagon. And for God's sake don't tell anybody we stayed here. Knowing this old moonshine-making wench, the word'll be all around the parish by sunup. We should have left home earlier.

PEARL: Lester, I don't care 'bout your reputation. Not when I'm about to vomit.

> *(PEARL runs from the room. We hear her gagging in the bedroom as thunder rolls and lightning flashes. LESTER takes a lamp and exits to the bedroom. As we hear the sound of a wagon driving up, PEARL screams)*

(Offstage) Shittt!!! Bedbugs!

TATE *(Offstage)*: Whoa! We rest here for the night.

> *(TATE enters with BUSHKIN, LILLY, and KITTY. TATE has a pistol on his side and BUSHKIN is in handcuffs. LILLY and KITTY carry a cloth suitcase)*

LILLY: I tell you I come from Charleston aristocracy and I detest this treatment, you bag of cow dung!

KITTY: We boog-wa-zees, you no-count piece of white trash. Tell him, Alex.

BUSHKIN: Ladies, please.

TATE: Ladies? Anytime two women are married to the same man at the same time, we call them whores down here.

BUSHKIN: I'll face your judge, Mr. Tate, and force him to strike from the record that archaic law . . . a man can have only one wife. I'm from a long line of fighting Russians and . . .

TATE: I don't give a shit if you from a long line of rattlesnakes. You gonna be facing the hanging judge. The meanest son of a bitch to ever put on a black robe. Hates everybody including his own mama. Gave his baby brother twenty years for stealing. When he gits through with you . . . we'll see 'bout your fancy words and highfalutin ways.

KITTY: His baby brother. His . . .

TATE: This is Ma Lola's place. We stay here for the night. I'll be in the barn watching 'case you get any ideas 'bout trying to beat the odds with them gators. If you run, I'll kill you. You know I will. (*Exits*)

LILLY: He smells like horses. And I seen him rubbing one of them mares we come on in a very familiar way.

(BUSHKIN *looks to see if* TATE *is gone. He comes back*)

BUSHKIN: You two are the dumbest, imbecilic, moronic . . .

KITTY: Don't you be using no fancy Russian words on me, Alex.

LILLY: It was her fault!

BUSHKIN: It was both your faults. I should have left you both in that sporting house in Charleston.

LILLY: You . . . you said you loved us both.

KITTY: You got no choice now. You married us. I got my papers to prove it.

LILLY: Me, too.

BUSHKIN: You two were in charge of the maps. How could I navigate the boat, read the maps, fuel the engine . . . I told you Utah. We could live together as man and wives in *Utah*.

KITTY: I thought it was Utah. I didn't know it was Louisiana! We shouldn't have stopped in that town for supplies.

BUSHKIN: What were we supposed to eat? The bark from trees?

KITTY: If you was half a man, you woulda caught us some rabbits to eat.

BUSHKIN: With my bare hands?

KITTY: My daddy did it.

BUSHKIN (*Engrossed in his own thoughts*):   My oldest brother, Peter . . . Peter can kill with his bare hands. Peter always had blood under his fingernails. When we were young my father would take us on hunts. For geese. Peter would wait very patiently near the pond. When the geese came, the sky would be black from their wings. They would light down. Suddenly Peter would pounce upon a poor unsuspecting bird! And as we all watched, he would break the poor bird's neck. And while the bird was still alive, Peter would pluck the feathers from its body as the poor thing screamed in pain. He would just pluck and laugh. Now it's my neck that he wants to break.

LILLY: He done flipped out if you ask me!

BUSHKIN: Tate, my God. Maybe Tate's from the party. They sent Tate to kill me. No, no, no, no . . .

KITTY: Alex, Alex, man, you got to get a grip on yourself!

BUSHKIN: Communist bastards. Long live the bourgeoisie! Long live—

LILLY: You just full of shit. Why don't you stop this play-acting and get us out of this fix? How the hell did I ever let you convince me you was a rich Russian prince?

> (*As* BUSHKIN *is about to enter the house,* MA *enters from stage right.* MA *has been in the barn talking to* TATE. MA *knows who* BUSHKIN, LILLY, *and* KITTY *are.* MA *gives* BUSHKIN *a disgusted look and enters the living room ahead of him. Lights come up to full on the living room as* BUSHKIN *enters behind* MA)

Who the hell are . . .

MA: You low-life, Godless things. Ain't y'all got one lick of common decency? Tate told me all about it. You ought to read your Bible. It speaks against what you're doing. And these two tramps. These harlots!

KITTY (*Standing*):   Now just a damn minit!

MA: Don't you bull up against me, girl, or I'll wear this furniture out with your hide. (*To* KITTY) Sit down. (KITTY *sits*) I never thought I'd see the day when my dear, sweet home would be shamed by your kind of horse manure. I can smell the stench clean out in the yard.

BUSHKIN: Madam, it's obvious you have a limited command of the English language, so I'll just pretend we aren't having this conversation.

MA: You kin pretend anything you want. But the judge's gonna hang you. He's a God-fearing man that hates Germans and fornicators. And from what I hear from Tate, you might be both.

BUSHKIN: I'm not Ger— Never mind.

MA: I got my buggy hitched up. I'm sleeping over to my sister's place tonight. The state pays me to put folks up traveling to court. That includes the likes of you. But I don't have to sleep under the same roof with you. And you'd better not get in my beds. You sleep out here. On the floor, on the ceiling, I don't care. Get in my beds and I'll shoot you.

BUSHKIN: Thank you for your strong sense of justice and fair play, madam.

> (MA *exits*)

Imbeciles, barbarians. I hate these mutants they call Southerners. But I'll live. Do you hear me, Peter? You'll never find me. Never. Ladies, never listen to your older brother, especially when he's the only one entrusted to run the family estate. You will lose every time. Lenin, my dear Kitty, has a wretched philosophy, and he uses men like Peter. And my dear, dear Lilly, I'm absolutely horrified that my family can no longer summer at St. Petersburg. They've taken the Baltic from me, too.

LILLY: Alex, you the sweetest-talking man I ever heard. Now most of it I know ain't worth two cents. But you got one more silver tongue in this world. You talked me out of sexual favors that I normally charge for. For you it was free.

KITTY: Done it to me, too.

LILLY: Oh God, you can talk about the moon and the stars so pretty that my garter belt will just melt right before my eyes.

> (*Suddenly* PEARL *runs through the room in her bathrobe.* PEARL *has a handful of newspapers*)

PEARL: The outhouse! Please let me make the outhouse! Don't stop me! Don't stop me!

> (PEARL *exits through the front door.* LESTER *enters half asleep as* PEARL *exits*)

LESTER: Watch out for black widow spiders, honey! That toilet seat's rickety! It's my destiny never to sleep again as long as I live on earth. (*Sees* BUSHKIN, KITTY, *and* LILLY) Who the kingdom come are you?

BUSHKIN: I'm Alex Bushkin, good sir, and these are . . . this is my wife Kitty and this is Lilly . . . a friend of the family. Yes, a dear friend.

LESTER: I'm Lester Simmons. That blur that just run through here was my wife, Pearl.

BUSHKIN: I heard her say something about another house.

LESTER: Outhouse. Ma Lola don't have no inside relief facilities.

KITTY: Wonderful.

LESTER: She's had stomach cramps something terrible for the past two days. God, please let me go to sleep. Cure my Pearl so I can get a decent night's rest.

BUSHKIN: Poor dear. I'm a doctor of sorts. Maybe I can do something for her. A remedy.

LILLY: Stay out of it, Alex. You're no . . .

(PEARL *slowly drags herself back in and sits in a rocker*)

PEARL: I'm gonna die this time, Lester. I know I'm gonna die.

(BUSHKIN *goes to his suitcase and brings out a bottle of medicine*)

BUSHKIN: I know stomach remedy, sir. My mother was from Georgia.

PEARL: So is mine. Atlanta.

BUSHKIN: No, no. On the Black Sea. In Caucasia . . . in . . . never mind. Here. Drink.

(PEARL *drinks from* BUSHKIN'*s bottle of medicine*)

PEARL: It's slimy.

BUSHKIN: It works.

PEARL: I hope so. Ain't much of my innards left.

LESTER: Thanks for the medicine, Mr. Bushkin.

BUSHKIN (*Looking at* PEARL):   My pleasure. Any flower will bloom and stand tall and fragrant like the majestic rose, given the proper nourishment and . . . remedy.

PEARL: You talking 'bout me?

LILLY: He's got a cure for everything. 'Cept a noose.

BUSHKIN: I don't have one for a lonely disenfranchised exile whose inhabitancy is now a foreign Southern, mosquito- and alligator-infested shore. Deprived of his homeland by Lenin and the Marxist . . . and oh, yes . . . his own dear brother.

> (PEARL *is now absorbed in* BUSHKIN'*s every word.* PEARL *looks at* BUSHKIN *with a lover's eyes.* LESTER *has fallen asleep standing up*)

His own brother who wanted power and position in the party so badly, being so seduced by this antibourgeois philosophy that he sacrificed the family's wealth. To the disenfranchisement of the poor foreigner! Fuck the Bolsheviks! Drink up!

PEARL: Good Lord! I wish Lester would talk to me like that. That was just marvelous, Mr. Bushkin.

KITTY (*Pointing to* LESTER):   Do Lester always sleep standing up?

> (*Pause.* PEARL *is looking at* BUSHKIN)

Well do he?

PEARL: Who, what, oh . . . yes.

LILLY: Looks like your hands is full tending to *your own* husband.

PEARL (*Shaking* LESTER):   Lester. Come on, honey. Wake up.

LESTER (*Waking up*):   Oh no, honey. Not again. I jest closed my eyes. You got to go again?

PEARL: Let's go to bed.

> (PEARL *leads* LESTER *out of the living room as her eyes are locked into* BUSHKIN's. PEARL *and* LESTER *exit to their bedroom*)

LILLY: That wench's got eyes for you, Alex.

BUSHKIN: Nonsense.

KITTY: She can do whatever she wants with her eyes. I'm gonna close mine and get some sleep. If those rednecks gonna hang us, I don't want to die with bags under my eyes.

> (KITTY *lies down on the floor to sleep.* LILLY *lies on the couch*)

LILLY: Guess I shouldda made me out a will.

> (*There is silence as* BUSHKIN *paces the floor*)

BUSHKIN: Think, Alexis. Think. There's got to be a way out of here. (*Goes to the window. He sees* TATE *standing guard.* BUSHKIN *leaves the window. Suddenly* PEARL *bolts out of the bedroom on her way to the outhouse*)

PEARL: Tell my husband . . . I died . . . on the toilet seat. Lester!

> (PEARL *screams and* LESTER *hears the scream. Again he is awakened.* LESTER *slowly enters the living room.* KITTY *and* LILLY *are startled by* PEARL's *scream*)

LILLY: The hell's going on?

BUSHKIN: My medicine worked.

KITTY: It did?

LESTER: It didn't! My wife's still got diarrhea.

BUSHKIN: But you said . . . she had stomach cramps.

LESTER: She do. Can't you see she do?

BUSHKIN: I . . . I treated her for . . . constipation.

LESTER: You what?

BUSHKIN: I . . . I . . . I gave her castor oil.

LESTER: You donkey's ass! You done killed my wife. (*Runs from the room to join* PEARL *at the outhouse*)

BUSHKIN: I'm cursed. Cursed! (*Looking toward heaven*) Am I never going to have good luck? Some good luck, please! Everything I touch just . . . dies. (*Runs to the window*) I know they're coming to kill me. They won't find me down here. No Russian in his right mind would travel this far south. But I must keep running . . . just in case.

> (LILLY *and* KITTY *lie down to sleep.* BUSHKIN *turns a quart bottle of vodka to his head. He runs over to the window and he looks out. He sees* LESTER *talking to* TATE. BUSHKIN *whispers to himself*)

He . . . he's talking to Tate! (*Leaves the window*) He knows. He knows about my wives. He knows who I am! How could he? Tate doesn't even know who I really am. (*Pauses, thinking. Talking quietly*) That's it. It's confirmed. The proletariat anarchist false leadership has sent Lester and Tate . . . to assassinate me. Pretend you don't know who he is when he comes back in and . . . beg for your life.

> (LESTER *slowly enters the house. He stops but doesn't look at* BUSHKIN. *Silence.* LESTER *has changed. He's now fully awake and there is menace in his voice*)

LESTER: Evil always overtakes me when the sky gets dark and cloudy. Thunder and lightning but no rain.

(*Silence*)

BUSHKIN (*Whispering aside*):   He's going to strike me. I can feel it. Delay the strike. Diverge. Diverge. (*To* LESTER) Yes . . . yes, Mr. Simmons. It does look like we're in for a rough storm.

LESTER: No. Sky's clear as a bell. Stars as bright as Aunt Flossie's gold teeth. Wolf moon, full and silvery.

(*Silence.* LESTER *continues to act mysterious, not looking at* BUSHKIN)

BUSHKIN: How . . . how's your wife . . . doing?

LESTER: Thanks to you, Mr. Bushkin, she's got to sleep sittin' on that toilet seat. I throwed a blanket over her . . . kissed her . . . due to space and the condition of the air, we both couldn't occupy Ma Lola's exterior convenience at the same time. But I'll check on her from time to time.

BUSHKIN: Sir. I'm sorry about the wrong remedy. I was only trying to help. I . . .

(KITTY *and* LILLY *sit up*)

LILLY (*To* BUSHKIN):   I told you to stay out of it.

LESTER: Oh, that's all right. It'll all come out in the wash.

BUSHKIN: The wash? Would you care for a drink? I . . . I've had more than my share. I'm starting to think dangerous thoughts. The liquid spirits are like that, you know.

LESTER: So is the ones made of flesh, you know. (*Looks at* BUSHKIN *and drinks from the bottle. Pause*)

BUSHKIN: Sir . . . have you been sent by the communists . . . to assassinate me?

LESTER: You got a dark, dark soul. So eat up with guilt and damnation that you think every shadow is the hangman's noose.

LILLY: And how would your soul feel if you had watched your brother pulling the bloody feathers from live gooses? And them damn things howling and screaming all over Russia from pain.

(*Pause*)

BUSHKIN: What did Tate tell you?

LESTER: Everything. You know we never stop here at Ma Lola's. That storm forcing us to stop here. Then it don't storm. You being here at the same time. It was divine intervention that brought us together. For what purpose, do you suppose?

BUSHKIN: Murder.

LESTER: No. Something higher than that. Judgment. You are a low, low, low, devil-infested, blasphemous bastard, Mr. Bushkin! Defying all of the natural laws of God and marrying two women! Bringing those harlots among the clean, chaste, undefiled people of this parish. What kind of heathen does that? One that should be punished! Flung out from among us! You're the devil! But we'll strike you down! Devil! Just fornicating all over our parish!

BUSHKIN: No, no, no! Listen to me, please. Lester, I can see that you're a compassionate, reasonable man.

LESTER: I been called worse.

BUSHKIN: You get angry. You lash out. That's good. It means you have conviction. Moral conviction.

LESTER: Boy, don't you talk to me 'bout morals. You one of them Mor-mons, ain't you?

BUSHKIN: I'm a Russian landowner.

LESTER: I'm John the Baptist.

BUSHKIN: It's true. I'm stranded here in this country. As you may have read . . . you *can* read, can't you?

LESTER: You'll know soon enough.

> (LILLY *and* KITTY *go to the window and look out. From the window we can see the sinister shadow of* TATE, *watching the house.* BUSHKIN *is now talking with the serious conviction of a man about to die, as he pleads to* LESTER *for help.* TATE's *shadow disappears from the window*)

BUSHKIN: Mr. Simmons, I'm on my way to face the hanging judge. A satanic man who's probably full of ignorance, hatred, and no concern for justice. I'm frightened . . . I'm desperate, Mr. Simmons. I need help. If I'm guilty of anything . . . which I'm not . . . it's the desire to live and see my country liberated from the communists. I no longer have a family to go back to. My oldest brother sold out to the Bolsheviks. Giving away to a bad, bad system all that we've worked for. They asked me to come home. "Join the party. There is a place for you, Alexis." I didn't go back. My father denounced the party. He's dead. My mother denounced . . . she's dead. I'm the only other heir left. And I know they want me dead. I have been running in fear of my life for the past year since they came to power. I don't want to be sent back. I can fight them better here. I did marry two wives. I was going to Utah to live as a Mormon. But not as an evil man. But a man determined to live and liberate his country. Who would ever suspect me as being Alexis Bushkenov in Utah, with two wives? No honest, respectable Russian would do that. I was buying time.

LESTER: Then you were using those poor, innocent little harlot angels . . . as a disguise!

BUSHKIN: Angels of mercy, Mr. Simmons. They are being used for a glorious cause.

LESTER: Well, least you ain't one of them Kaiser Germans.

BUSHKIN: I denounce the Kaiser and I praise democracy's victorious victory in the Great War. (*Takes a drink*) Salud!

(LESTER *is caught up in the moment*)

LILLY (*At the window*):   Tate's disappeared.

LESTER: Yes, yes. Mine eyes have seen the glory! Sal-lud! (*Drinks. Pause*) You telling me the truth?

BUSHKIN: Yes, I am. And since we've been married . . . the ladies and I . . . we've never had sexual intercourse. Thanks to jealousy. I did pay for their sexual favors when they worked the Scarlet Garter in Charleston. But I swear to you, oh righteous sir . . . we never fornicated in this parish. (*Pause*) Please. Please help us. I don't want to die. Hanging is the worst. Please?

LESTER: I'll think on it.

BUSHKIN: I don't have a lot of time. When Tate comes for us . . . it's the end.

(*Silence as the two men look at each other.* LESTER *exits to his bedroom. After several beats,* PEARL *walks in zombielike.* PEARL *looks straight ahead*)

How . . . how do you feel?

PEARL: My behind's chafed beyond recognition. Musta been the newspaper print. Sears is usually softer, too.

(*Exits to her bedroom*)

BUSHKIN: If this is a bad dream, it's gone on far too long. That's it. Close my eyes and scream . . . wake up! Wake up! Wake . . . up!

(MA LOLA *and* TATE *enter.* MA LOLA *is holding a shotgun.* TATE *is carrying a hangman's rope*)

What . . . what are you doing? You can't do . . .

MA: Yes, we can. We ain't got to take you all the way to Baton Rouge. The judge sent Tate to get me over at my sister's. He wanted an impartial witness. Even though it's one hour 'fore rooster crow, the news sprung me wide awake.

TATE: You done been tried and we got the tree waiting.

BUSHKIN: We haven't been tried! What you're doing is illegal! We are entitled to a trial before a judge.

(LESTER *enters dressed in a black judge's robe.* PEARL *enters behind him*)

TATE: All rise. Judge Lester A. Simmons presiding.

BUSHKIN: You? You're the hanging judge? The one we're . . .

LILLY: Shit.

KITTY: Shit. Shit.

TATE: Will the accused please be seated?

KITTY: That's us, I reckon.

(BUSHKIN, KITTY, *and* LILLY *sit*)

LESTER: Will Alexis Bushkenov please rise.

(BUSHKIN *stands*)

BUSHKIN: Lester . . . Sorry. Your Honor. You haven't given us a fair trial.

LESTER: I've been trying you all night. Twenty years they've called me a hangman. I only listen to legal facts. The law. The law is the hangman. I'm only the administrator of the law and justice. I figured that I'd try a different tactic tonight, since fate had consciously thrown the judge and the accused into this strange arena of justice. I find judging with the heart a mite more interesting than judging with the legal facts. I see standing and sitting before me three of earth's lowest dogs. Driven by demons into sin and fornication. But . . . they're not Germans. This man is a liar and a deceiver, but . . . he loves democracy and he hates the Kaiser. He's given to strong drink, but . . . he's considerate of these two whores. And, yes, my darling wife, who he thought to be constipated. He's ignorant, I'll admit, but that's not his fault. He comes from a backward country of Russian infidels. May God have mercy on their souls and may they burn in hell. Until I met the accused, I'd never seen a human being grovel so and crawl on his belly, eyes filled with tears and begging for mercy. It was a beautiful sight. He has a mission in life which this court finds honorable and Christian. And he's convinced the court that he's not fornicated within the confines of this parish. (*Pause*) I ain't had a good hanging in twenty-two days.

TATE: Sir, you ain't thinking 'bout lettin' these snakes go, are you? I spent good time fixin' this noose, judge. You can't cheat me like that.

MA: We need a good hanging, Your Honor.

LESTER: I suppose I'm gettin' too soft for the job. Court . . . adjourned.

BUSHKIN: Thank you, sir! Thank you! From the bottom of my heart. Thank you! May I kiss your boots?

LESTER: If I catch you and these two buzzard baits in Louisiana again, well, I'll just kill you on sight. No trial.

BUSHKIN: Oh, no. Never again, sir. Never. (*Looks at* KITTY *and* LILLY)

LILLY: Never.

KITTY: In life. I promise on all that's sacred.

(LESTER *exits*. PEARL *looks back at* BUSHKIN. *Then she exits*)

TATE (*Disappointedly*):   I'm going . . . I don't know. Maybe I'll leave Louisiana altogether. Go where people believe in justice. Goodbye, Ma. I shore wanted to see somebody die. (*Exits*)

MA: I'm gonna burn my house down to the ground as a sacrifice to the defiling of the Holy Covenant.

BUSHKIN: I can assure you, my lady, we're not that important.

MA: Never thought I'd see the day Lester'd git soft in the head. Broke my heart, Lester. I'm gonna spend my last days at my sister's.

KITTY: What we gonna do now?

BUSHKIN: We are man and wives, but if you want to break the vows, I'll understand.

KITTY: Break . . . man, it was you who was playing them games. I don't want to break no vows. Do you know how hard a good, intelligent man is to come by? You the catch of the year!

LILLY: I'll be headin' back to South Carolina.

BUSHKIN: You'll be heading to Utah with your husband. Unless . . . well . . . you just have to.

LILLY: Utah'd be more interesting, although I know I'm gonna have to scratch Kitty's eyes out.

KITTY: Try it!

BUSHKIN: Ladies . . . ladies. Let's just get our bag and leave. Fast!

KITTY: We already packed. I'll git the bag.

LILLY: I'll help.

(*As* BUSHKIN *is preparing to leave,* PEARL *tiptoes into the room with her suitcase. In the distance we hear a rooster crowing in the dawn*)

KITTY: What you sniffing around for?

BUSHKIN: Mrs. Simmons.

PEARL: Call me Pearl. I'm going with ya.

BUSHKIN: You what?! Your husband will . . .

PEARL: Sleep till noon. It's 'bout daylight now. So we'll git a big head start on him. We'll just git on your boat and head out.

BUSHKIN: But why?

PEARL: Well . . . both our families from Georgia. And I believe in the bond of names. No matter how different the location on earth. It's a sign. You was sent as a sign to me and . . . I want to help you retake Russia. I do.

BUSHKIN: But you can't go with us . . .

PEARL: You ain't got no choice. If I tell my husband you asked me for favors of my flesh, ain't *nobody* gonna leave.

BUSHKIN: You wouldn't.

PEARL: The hell I won't. I am sick and tired of this place, and you my last hope. And I want to be one of your *wives* . . . comrade!

BUSHKIN: No!

KITTY/LILLY: What?

LILLY: The hell you will. Me and Kitty ain't sharing this man!

BUSHKIN (*To* LILLY):   Ssssh! You want to wake up the judge? Mrs. Simmons, what you're doing is called *blackmail*.

PEARL: I know what it's called. But you done messed around and made me fall in love with you. I never heard a man talk as sweet as you in my entire life. You make this majestic rose blossom just wilt under your power.

KITTY: Cactus plant, is more like it.

BUSHKIN (*To* KITTY *and* LILLY):   We don't have a choice. (*To* PEARL) You want to be my . . .

PEARL: Wife! (*Picks up her bag and tiptoes out the door*)

BUSHKIN/LILLY/KITTY (*To the audience*):   Three?!

A Joke

It was noon of a bright winter's day. The air was crisp with frost, and Nadia, who was walking beside me, found her curls and the delicate down on her upper lip silvered with her own breath. We stood at the summit of a high hill. The ground fell away at our feet in a steep incline which reflected the sun's rays like a mirror. Near us lay a little sled brightly upholstered with red.

"Let us coast down, Nadia!" I begged. "Just once! I promise you nothing will happen."

But Nadia was timid. The long slope, from where her little overshoes were planted to the foot of the ice-clad hill, looked to her like the wall of a terrible, yawning chasm. Her heart stopped beating, and she held her breath as she gazed into that abyss while I urged her to take her seat on the sled. What might not happen were she to risk a flight over that precipice! She would die, she would go mad!

"Come, I implore you!" I urged her again. "Don't be afraid! It is cowardly to fear, to be timid."

At last Nadia consented to go, but I could see from her face that she did so, she thought, at the peril of her life. I seated her, all pale and trembling, in the little sled, put my arm around her, and together we plunged into the abyss.

The sled flew like a shot out of a gun. The riven wind lashed our faces; it howled and whistled in our ears, and plucked furiously at us, trying to wrench our heads from our shoulders; its pressure stifled us; we felt as if the devil himself had seized us in his talons, and were snatching us with a shriek down into the infernal regions. The objects on either hand melted into a long and madly flying streak. Another second, and it seemed we must be lost!

"I love you, Nadia!" I whispered.

And now the sled began to slacken its pace, the howling of the wind and the swish of the runners sounded less terrible, we breathed again, and found ourselves at the foot of the mountain at last. Nadia, more dead than alive, was breathless and pale. I helped her to her feet.

"Not for anything in the world would I do that again!" she said, gazing at me with wide, terror-stricken eyes. "Not for anything on earth. I nearly died!"

In a few minutes, however, she was herself again, and already her inquiring eyes were asking the question of mine:

"Had I really uttered those four words, or had she only fancied she heard them in the tumult of the wind?"

I stood beside her smoking a cigarette and looking attentively at my glove.

She took my arm and we strolled about for a long time at the foot of the hill. It was obvious that the riddle gave her no peace. Had I spoken those words or not? It was for her a question of pride, of honor, of happiness, of life itself, a very important question, the most important one in the whole world. Nadia looked at me now impatiently, now sorrowfully, now searchingly; she answered my questions at random and waited for me to speak. Oh, what a pretty play of expression flitted across her sweet face! I saw that she was struggling with herself; she longed to say something, to ask some question, but the words would not come; she was terrified and embarrassed and happy.

"Let me tell you something," she said, without looking at me.

"What?" I asked.

"Let us—let us slide down the hill again!"

We mounted the steps that led to the top of the hill. Once more I seated Nadia, pale and trembling, in the little sled; once more we plunged into that terrible abyss; once more the wind howled, and the runners hissed; and once more, at the wildest and most tumultuous moment of our descent, I whispered:

"I love you, Nadia!"

When the sleigh had come to a standstill, Nadia threw a backward look at the hill down which we had just sped, and then gazed for a long time into my face, listening to the calm, even tones of my voice. Every inch of her, even her muff and her hood, every line of her little frame expressed the utmost uncertainty. On her face was written the question:

"What can it have been? Who spoke those words? Was it he, or was it only my fancy?"

The uncertainty of it was troubling her, and her patience was becoming exhausted. The poor girl had stopped answering my questions, she was pouting and ready to cry.

"Had we not better go home?" I asked.

"I—I love coasting!" she answered with a blush. "Shall we not slide down once more?"

She "loved" coasting, and yet, as she took her seat on the sled, she was as trembling and pale as before and scarcely could breathe for terror!

We coasted down for the third time and I saw her watching my face and following the movements of my lips with her eyes. But I put my handkerchief to my mouth and coughed, and when we were halfway down I managed to say:

"I love you, Nadia!"

So the riddle remained unsolved! Nadia was left pensive and silent. I escorted her home, and as she walked she shortened her steps and tried to go slowly, waiting for me to say those words. I was aware of the struggle going on in her breast, and of how she was forcing herself not to exclaim:

"The wind could not have said those words! I don't want to think that it said them!"

Next day I received the following note:

"If you are going coasting today, call for me. N."

Thenceforth Nadia and I went coasting every day, and each time that we sped down the hill on our little sled I whispered the words:

"I love you, Nadia!"

Nadia soon grew to crave this phrase as some people crave morphine or wine. She could no longer live without hearing it! Though to fly down the hill was as terrible to her as ever, danger and fear lent a strange fascination to those words of love, words which remained a riddle to torture her heart. Both the wind and I were suspected; which of us two was confessing our love for her now seemed not to matter; let the draft but be hers, and she cared not for the goblet that held it!

One day, at noon, I went to our hill alone. There I perceived Nadia. She approached the hill, seeking me with her eyes, and at last I saw her timidly mounting the steps that led to the summit. Oh, how fearful, how terrifying she found it to make that journey alone! Her face was as white as the snow, and she shook as if she were going to her doom, but up she climbed, firmly, without one backward look. Clearly she had determined to discover once for all whether those wondrously sweet words would reach her ears if I was not there. I saw her seat herself on the sled with a pale face and lips parted with horror, saw her shut her eyes and push off, bidding farewell forever to this world. "Zzzzzzz!" hissed the runners. What did she hear? I know not—I only saw her rise tired and trembling from the sled, and it was clear from her expression that she could not herself have said what she had heard; on her downward rush terror had robbed her of the power of distinguishing the sounds that came to her ears.

And now, with March, came the spring. The sun's rays grew warmer and brighter. Our snowy hillside grew darker and duller, and the ice crust finally melted away. Our coasting came to an end.

Nowhere could poor Nadia now hear the beautiful words, for there was no one to say them; the wind was silent and I was preparing to go to St. Petersburg for a long time, perhaps forever.

One evening, two days before my departure, I sat in the twilight in a little garden separated from the garden where Nadia lived by a high fence surmounted by iron spikes. It was cold and the snow was still on the ground, the trees were lifeless, but the scent of spring was in the air, and the rooks were cawing noisily as they settled themselves for the night. I approached the fence, and for a long time peered through a chink in the boards. I saw Nadia come out of the house and stand on the doorstep, gazing with anguish and longing at the sky. The spring wind was blowing directly into her pale, sorrowful face. It reminded her of the wind that had howled for us on the hillside when she had heard those four words, and with that recollection her face grew very sad indeed, and the tears rolled down her cheeks. The poor child held out her arms as if to implore the wind to bring those words to her ears once more. And I, waiting for a gust to carry them to her, said softly:

"I love you, Nadia!"

Heavens, what an effect my words had on Nadia! She cried out and stretched forth her arms to the wind, blissful, radiant, beautiful. . . .

And I went to pack up my things. All this happened a long time ago. Nadia married, whether for love or not matters little. Her husband is an official of the nobility, and she now has three children. But she has not forgotten how we coasted together and how the wind whispered to her:

"I love you, Nadia!"

That memory is for her the happiest, the most touching, the most beautiful one of her life.

But as for me, now that I have grown older, I can no longer understand why I said those words and why I jested with Nadia.

The Talking Dog

by

JOHN GUARE

CHARACTERS

F   *She is in her twenties.*

M   *He is in his late twenties.*

                       Each of them wears a white jumpsuit.

HANG-GLIDER #1   *Each of them wears a brightly colored*
HANG-GLIDER #2   *jumpsuit and black-lensed goggles.*

A bare stage. White.

F: Hang-gliding!

M: Hang-gliding.

F: I don't understand anything *about* hang-gliding!

M: You wear this harness—

F: You don't understand—

M: You insert yourself into the machine—

F: I am a complete coward—

M: The wings—the sails—the structure takes care of every-thing—

F: All I have to do is jump off the mountain. Look at it down there! It's miles—don't get too close! Watch out for the edge! Oh dear God, I am not religious and I am praying! You have me praying! This goddam mountain—

M: This is not a mountain.

F: That's right. Don't pay any attention to my nosebleed or the thin air or the birds flying below us—the birds have nosebleeds!

M: This is the Catskills.

F: The Catskills *are* mountains. The Catskills are not Death Valley turned upside down. The Catskills are not the Gobi Desert.

M: The Alps are mountains. The Himalayas are mountains.

F: And the Catskills—

M: —are the Catskills. You just strap on your machine and step over the edge.

F: Be careful!

M: Feel the air. The wind. The purity. Breathe deep!

F: And you like to do this?

M: It's what you said about courage.

F: Courage.

M: We have to give ourselves tests of courage all the time to grow, to know we're progressing.

F: Stepping off a mountain is not a progression. Except one way. The air is too thin here. I want to be taken down. By a car. On a road.

M: Don't you want to appear worthwhile to yourself? Don't you want to know you're strong? That you have the strength for life? You have to grow, and the best way to grow—

F: Is not to jump off a mountain—

M: Is by a simple act of courage. And you're protected. You stretch out in the machine. These ropes operate the struts, the wings. You actually control the wind. Mastery over nature! You control the invisible! That which is invisible holds you up. It is impossible to plummet. You are safer in this glider than you are, say, crossing Fifth Avenue. The wind catches you, supports you, welcomes you. A baby could be put in this and glide to earth as safely as Moses drifting in the bulrushes.

F: If I had a baby, I would not let it hang-glide. Moses or not.

M *(Sings lightly, seductively)*:   Rockabye baby
In the tree top
When the wind blows
The cradle will rock—

F: The cradle will *drop*. Drop rhymes with top. Down will come baby, cradle, and all—

M: Just strap the harness on.

      (HANG-GLIDER #1 *in his bright-colored jumpsuit comes to* HER. HANG-GLIDER *stands waiting, expectantly, good-natured, arms outstretched, welcoming, wearing black-lensed goggles.* SHE *backs away.* SHE *looks over the edge*)

F: I land down there?

M: You land down there.

F: How long?

M: Does it take?

F: How long does it take?

M: It can be over in a few minutes.

F: No!

M: Or if you're good—

F: I want to be good.

M: It can take . . . oh, you can prolong it, prolong the flight, extend the voyage for as long as you can keep control, feel the desire, control the wind, find new bits of current. Slow. Slow. Slow.

F: What's the longest you've ever stayed up?

M: Once—almost an hour.

F: An hour!

M: Generally thirty minutes.

F: You're good.

M: I'm good.

F: Courage.

M: Courage.

F: Were you afraid at first?

M: Everybody is.

F: I want to be strong.

M: Then just do it. You're not alone. Look down there.

F: Other people leaping off the cliffs. Filling the air.

M: This is the hang-gliding capital of the world.

F: I don't see anybody plunging down.

M: They gave you the lesson.

F: We paid the money.

M: I'll fly right beside you.

F: The wind is so high.

M (*Testing the wind*):   If it wasn't—ahh, then I'd be worried.

F: And you're not frightened.

M: Just that little edge in the stomach—that one frightened edge to conquer.

F: We strap ourselves in and go?

M: Yes.

> (SHE *adjusts her harness.* SHE *stands with her back to* HANG-GLIDER #1. HANG-GLIDER *attaches her harness to the strap on his chest.* HANG-GLIDER *lifts* HER. SHE *wraps her legs around* HANG-GLIDER's *waist and extends her arms out in front of her, her back arched, her stomach parallel to the ground.*
> M *puts on his helmet.* HE *puts her helmet on her head and kisses her hands, which* SHE *puts into a prayer position.*
> HANG-GLIDER #2 *appears in his brightly colored jumpsuit and black goggles.* M *quickly and expertly adjusts his straps onto* HANG-GLIDER's *chest.* HANG-GLIDER #2 *hikes up* M, *who wraps his legs around* HANG-GLIDER's *waist, and confidently stretches out his arms, his back arched, his stomach parallel to the ground.*
> THE HANG-GLIDERS *walk their two passengers to the back of the playing area.* M *and* F *stand side by side.* HE *raises his hand*)

M: Ten.

F: Nine.

M: Eight.

F: Oh dear God.

M: EIGHT.

F: Seven.

M: Six.

F: Five.

M: Four.

F: I can't.

M: FOUR.

F: Three.

M: Two.

F: One.

> (*And* THEY *step forward, their arms extended like wings. The sound of wind.* SHE *screams.* THEY *crisscross each other, swooping around the stage, up, down, free. Delight*)

I'm doing it! I am not believing this! I am doing, actually doing, look at me doing this! Do you see me?

M: I.
    Love.
    You.

> (F *is silent for a moment, not sure of what she's heard.* SHE *lifts off her helmet and cranes her head.* M *signals her wildly to put her helmet back on, which she does.*
> THE HANG-GLIDERS *bring them to earth, detaching their harnesses.* HE *rolls and rolls over and over and jumps up vigorously, breathing heavily, excitedly, pulling off his helmet.* F *is exhausted.* SHE *sits in a heap, strangely troubled*)

Did—did you like it?

F (*Deep breaths*): I've never been more scared—that's a fact. I'm shaking. My breath. I'm afraid to feel my pulse.

M: Your pulse is fine.

F: You didn't tell me I'd have to use all my muscles. The power in the wind. It's not a free ride. There's no ground below you. The psychic shock. I'm in a sweat. The wind is so powerful.

M: Did you think you'd just move your pinky one way and the wind does this and you flick your wrist the other and the wind does that? All the reading. Lessons. Nothing prepares you for the power.

F: Or the sounds.

M: The sounds?

F: I thought I heard something.

M: Heard what?

F: Could—could we try it again?

>   (SHE *signals.* THE HANG-GLIDERS *reappear*)

M: I thought you didn't like it. The absence of earth. No terra firma. Only terror . . .

F: But if you did it with me . . .

>   (SHE *looks at him.* THEY *put on their helmets. Facing each other,* THEY *attach themselves to* THE HANG-GLIDERS *once more, and go to the back of the playing area.*
>   THEY *step forward.* THEY *swoop through space. The sound of the wind.* THEY *crisscross back and forth, their arms extended*)

M: I.
     Love.
     You.

>   (SHE *looks up eagerly.* THEY *land.* SHE *rolls over this time more confidently.* SHE *leaps up*)

F: Again!

M: There's a long line. There's rentals. It's by the hour.

F: Again. Again. Again. Again. Again.

M: There's money.

F: Again.

M: There's time. I have to get back to work.

F: Again.

M: You have to get back to work.

F: When can we do it again?

> (SHE *puts on her helmet.* HE *puts on his helmet.* THEY *attach themselves to their* HANG-GLIDERS *and swoop over the stage, whooping joyously*)

M: I.
Love.
You.

> (THEY *land on earth.* SHE *pulls off her helmet and looks at him expectantly*)

Yes?

F: Don't you want to say—something?

M: Say something? Like what?

> (SHE *steps back.* SHE *studies him.* HE *stands there smiling, puzzled.* HE *and* HANG-GLIDER #2 *back away*)

Like what?

> (SHE *is alone with* HANG-GLIDER #1. SHE *waits expectantly, checking her watch.* SHE *puts on her helmet.* SHE *attaches herself to* HANG-GLIDER #1, *goes to the back of the playing area, and steps forward, her arms outstretched in space.* SHE *glides.* HE *watches secretly, stifling laughter.* SHE *listens. Silence.* SHE *lands.* M *runs out to her*)

Solo!

F: Where were you?

M: Got stuck in traffic.

F: I waited. Come up with me?

M: I hurt my knee.

F: You didn't hurt your knee.

M: I can't go up. What? Do you think I'm joking? I hurt my knee. The Catskills are the home of the Borscht Belt comedians, but I'm no Catskill comic. I hurt my knee.

F: Are you serious?

M: Of course I'm serious. Why wouldn't I be serious?

F: Do you ever hear voices?

M: Like Joan of Arc? Joan of Arc of the Catskills? Now that's funny.

F: Do you believe Nature ever talks to us?

M: Nature ever talks to us?

F: Nature ever breaks its silence and speaks to us?

M (*Stifling laughter*):   What does Nature have to say to me?

F: To get us . . . to get us to join her.

M: Her?

F: I don't mean *Her* in a feminist way. I don't mean Her. But I don't really mean *Him*. Nature enlisting us, calling us to join— it's not *It*.

M: Pantheism?

F: Not pantheism because it's not God. I've never used the word "pantheism" in a sentence, so it's a shame it's not the right word, but it's more—

M: Songs like "The Breeze and I"? "I Talk to the Trees"?

F: No . . . maybe yes . . .

M: And what is Nature saying?

F: Don't you know?

M (*Stifling laughter*):   I just want to get this straight. Are you saying you have heard Nature speaking? This is very fascinating.

F: Have you ever heard it? That's all I'm asking.

M: Are you setting forth a theory or speaking about fact?

F: Could we go up for another ride?

M: My knee.

F: Your knee.

M: I'll hate it when winter comes and the snow and we can't do
this.

F: Skiing?

M: Skiing's not the same. Gliding. The air. The height.

F: Just once more?

> (THE HANG-GLIDERS *lift* M *and* F *up and carry them around
> once more.* SHE *listens.* HE *is silent.* THEY *land.* THE HANG-
> GLIDERS *retreat*)

I guess . . . no, just a theory . . . a dopey . . .

M: Oh, theory. I'm not good on theory. I'm a reality kind of guy.

F: Yes. Reality.

M: I had—I don't know what makes me think of this—but I
had this friend once who could train animals. She was a great
trainer of anything animal. The *National Geographic* offered her
lifetime contracts and unlimited expense accounts and intro-
ductions to safaris all over the world. And Viola had this Alaskan husky. White. Hairy. Blue glassy eyes of a wolf. And the

first time I went to her house to pick her up, I rang the door-
bell. The door opens and there is this great Alaskan husky
sitting down on its haunches, tail flapping away making this
thud thud thud on the hooked rug, and Fido puts up its
haunches and says (*Makes a growling noise like a hound baying*):

> I
> Love
> You

F: The husky talked?

M: Viola trained Fido—trained this Alaskan wolf—to turn its
growl into this sound:

> Hello
> I
> Love
> You

Well, Viola stepped around the door and flashed a flashbulb
taking my photo, the look of shock on my kisser. She loved to
take photos of people's faces when they heard this husky talk.

F: Why?

M: A joke. It made her very popular. People would come from
various nations to hear the dog talk.

> Hello
> I
> Love
> You

People would swear off alcohol and drugs or else take *up* alco-
hol and drugs. This dog would look at you with its vaguely
Oriental eyes of such intelligence and the growl
Hello
You'd think you'd gone over the hill . . . the edge . . . Don't
you think that's funny?

F: Well . . . she went to a lot of effort.

M: That was Viola.

F: What happened to Viola?

M: I don't know. The jungles. Talking alligators.

                         Hello
                         I
                         Lo—

I'm . . . I should tell you. I'm being transferred. Moving to
another coast. Well, more towards the middle of the country.
But a transfer. You really are terrific, how good you've become. It's really rewarding to see . . . and that sense of courage
. . . that . . .

> (M *has backed offstage as* HE *talks and is gone.* F *sits by herself,
> at a loss.* M *appears at the back of the stage, tiptoeing on very
> quietly.* HE *calls out softly*)

                         I
                         Love
                         You

> (HE *stifles a laugh as* SHE *sits up, listening*)

                         I
                         Love
                         You

> (SHE *is amazed.* SHE *holds her arms out to infinity, smiling. The
> lights begin to fade on her.* HE *comes forward and speaks to us*)

So I moved away. Transferred to another city, but I always
check into New York with the Sunday papers and I saw one
Sunday not long ago that she—that she was engaged to some
nerd. With a name like Casper. Or Rufus. Some stupid cretin-
ous name. Or else she married him. That page where it's all
weddings and engagements and plans for the future. That

page. I don't envy Rufus. Or Casper. I mean, she was a—grew
into a great hang-glider. Well, an adequate hang-glider, but I
don't think she was too much in the sense of humor department. Poor Rufus. Poor Casper. Living with somebody who
couldn't take a joke. This is years ago now . . . (*In his dog voice*)

> Hello
>
> I
>
> Love
>
> You

I mean, if I couldn't live with somebody like Viola—well,
aside from her dog, Viola had no sense of humor whatsoever,
but aside from that, I'd just as soon live alone as live with
somebody who couldn't take a

> take a
>
> take a (M *imitates a broken record*)
>
> take a
>
> joke.

The Witch

It was approaching nightfall. The sexton, Savély Gykin, was lying in his huge bed in the hut adjoining the church. He was not asleep, though it was his habit to go to sleep at the same time as the hens. His coarse red hair peeped from under one end of the greasy patchwork quilt, made up of colored rags, while his big unwashed feet stuck out from the other. He was listening. His hut adjoined the wall that encircled the church and the solitary window in it looked out upon the open country. And out there a regular battle was going on. It was hard to say who was being wiped off the face of the earth, and for the sake of whose destruction nature was being churned up into such a ferment; but, judging from the unceasing malignant roar, someone was getting it very hot. A victorious force was in full chase over the fields, storming in the forest and on the church roof, battering spitefully with its fists upon the windows, raging and tearing, while something vanquished was howling and wailing. . . . A plaintive lament sobbed at the window, on the roof, or in the stove. It sounded not like a call for help, but like a cry of misery, a consciousness that it was too late, that there was no salvation. The snowdrifts were covered with a thin coating of ice; tears quivered on them and on the trees; a dark slush of mud and melting snow flowed along the roads and paths. In short, it was thawing, but through the dark night the heavens failed to see it, and flung flakes of fresh snow upon the melting earth at a terrific rate. And the wind staggered like a drunkard. It would not let the snow settle on the ground, and whirled it around in the darkness at random.

Savély listened to all this din and frowned. The fact was that he knew, or at any rate suspected, what all this racket outside the window was tending to and whose handiwork it was.

"I know!" he muttered, shaking his finger menacingly under the bedclothes; "I know all about it."

On a stool by the window sat the sexton's wife, Raïssa Nilovna. A tin lamp standing on another stool, as though timid and distrustful of its powers, shed a dim and flickering light on her broad shoulders, on the handsome, tempting-looking contours of her person, and on her thick plait, which reached to the floor. She was making sacks out of coarse hempen stuff. Her hands moved nimbly, while her whole body, her eyes, her eyebrows, her full lips, her white neck were as still as though they were asleep, absorbed in the monotonous, mechanical toil. Only from time to time she raised her head to rest her weary neck, glanced for a moment towards the window, beyond which the snowstorm was raging, and bent again over her sacking. No desire, no joy, no grief, nothing was expressed by her handsome face with its turned-up nose and its dimples. So a beautiful fountain expresses nothing when it is not playing.

But at last she had finished a sack. She flung it aside, and, stretching luxuriously, rested her motionless, lackluster eyes on the window. The panes were swimming with drops like tears, and white with short-lived snowflakes which fell on the window, glanced at Raïssa, and melted. . . .

"Come to bed!" growled the sexton. Raïssa remained mute. But suddenly her eyelashes flickered and there was a gleam of attention in her eye. Savély, all the time watching her expression from under the quilt, put out his head and asked:

"What is it?"

"Nothing. . . . I fancy someone's coming," she answered quietly.

The sexton flung the quilt off with his arms and legs, knelt up in bed, and looked blankly at his wife. The timid light of the lamp illuminated his hirsute, pock-marked countenance and glided over his rough matted hair.

"Do you hear?" asked his wife.

Through the monotonous roar of the storm he caught a scarcely audible thin and jingling monotone like the shrill note of a gnat when it wants to settle on one's cheek and is angry at being prevented.

"It's the post," muttered Savély, squatting on his heels.

Two miles from the church ran the posting road. In windy weather, when the wind was blowing from the road to the church, the inmates of the hut caught the sound of bells.

"Lord! Fancy people wanting to drive about in such weather," sighed Raïssa.

"It's government work. You've to go whether you like or not."

The murmur hung in the air and died away.

"It has driven by," said Savély, getting into bed.

But before he had time to cover himself up with the bedclothes he heard a distinct sound of the bell. The sexton looked anxiously at his wife, leapt out of bed and walked, waddling, to and fro by the stove. The bell went on ringing for a little, then died away again as though it had ceased.

"I don't hear it," said the sexton, stopping and looking at his wife with his eyes screwed up.

But at that moment the wind rapped on the window and with it floated a shrill jingling note. Savély turned pale, cleared his throat, and flopped about the floor with his bare feet again.

"The postman is lost in the storm," he wheezed out, glancing malignantly at his wife. "Do you hear? The postman has lost his way! . . . I . . . I know! Do you suppose I . . . don't understand?" he muttered. "I know all about it, curse you!"

"What do you know?" Raïssa asked quietly, keeping her eyes fixed on the window.

"I know that it's all your doing, you she-devil! Your doing, damn you! This snowstorm and the post going wrong, you've done it all—you!"

"You're mad, you silly," his wife answered calmly.

"I've been watching you for a long time past and I've seen it. From the first day I married you I noticed that you'd bitch's blood in you!"

"Tfoo!" said Raïssa, surprised, shrugging her shoulders and crossing herself. "Cross yourself, you fool!"

"A witch is a witch," Savély pronounced in a hollow, tearful voice, hurriedly blowing his nose on the hem of his shirt; "though you are my wife, though you are of a clerical family, I'd say what you are even at confession. . . . Why, God have mercy upon us! Last year on the Eve of the Prophet Daniel and the Three Young Men there was a snowstorm, and what happened then? The mechanic came in to warm himself. Then on St. Alexey's Day the ice broke on the river and the district policeman turned up, and he was chatting with you all night . . . the damned brute! And when he came out in the morning and I looked at him, he had rings under his eyes and his cheeks were hollow! Eh? During the August fast there were two storms and each time the huntsman turned up. I saw it all, damn him! Oh, she is redder than a crab now, aha!"

"You didn't see anything."

"Didn't I! And this winter before Christmas on the Day of the Ten Martyrs of Crete, when the storm lasted for a whole day and night—do you remember?—the marshal's clerk was lost, and turned up here, the hound. . . . Tfoo! To be tempted by the clerk! It was worth upsetting God's weather for him! A driveling scribbler, not a foot from the ground, pimples all over his mug and his neck awry! If he were good-looking, anyway—but he, tfoo! He is as ugly as Satan!"

The sexton took a breath, wiped his lips, and listened. The bell was not to be heard, but the wind banged on the roof, and again there came a tinkle in the darkness.

"And it's the same thing now!" Savély went on. "It's not for nothing the postman is lost! Blast my eyes if the postman isn't looking for you! Oh, the devil is a good hand at his work; he is a fine one to help! He will turn him around and around and bring him here. I know, I see! You can't conceal it, you devil's bauble, you heathen wanton! As soon as the storm began I knew what you were up to."

"Here's a fool!" smiled his wife. "Why, do you suppose, you thick-head, that I make the storm?"

"Hmm! . . . Grin away! Whether it's your doing or not, I only know that when your blood's on fire there's sure to be bad weather, and when there's bad weather there's bound to be some crazy fellow turning up here. It happens so every time! So it must be you!"

To be more impressive the sexton put his finger to his forehead, closed his left eye, and said in a singsong voice:

"Oh, the madness! oh, the unclean Judas! If you really are a human being and not a witch, you ought to think what if he is not the mechanic, or the clerk, or the huntsman, but the devil in their form! Ah! You'd better think of that!"

"Why, you are stupid, Savély," said his wife, looking at him compassionately. "When father was alive and living here, all sorts of people used to come to him to be cured of the ague: from the village, and the hamlets, and the Armenian settlement. They came almost every day, and no one called them devils. But if anyone once a year comes in bad weather to warm himself, you wonder at it, you silly, and take all sorts of notions into your head at once."

His wife's logic touched Savély. He stood with his bare feet wide apart, bent his head, and pondered. He was not firmly convinced yet of the truth of his suspicions, and his wife's genuine and unconcerned tone quite disconcerted him. Yet after a moment's thought he wagged his head and said:

"It's not as though they were old men or bandylegged cripples; it's always young men who want to come for the night. . . . Why is that? And if they only wanted to warm themselves— But they are up to mischief. No, woman; there's no creature in this world as cunning as your female sort! Of real brains you've not an ounce, less than a starling, but for devilish slyness—oo-oo-oo! The Queen of Heaven protect us! There is the postman's bell! When the storm was only beginning I knew all that was in your mind. That's your witchery, you spider!"

"Why do you keep on at me, you heathen?" His wife lost her patience at last. "Why do you keep sticking to it like pitch?"

"I stick to it because if anything—God forbid—happens tonight . . . do you hear? . . . if anything happens tonight, I'll go straight off tomorrow morning to Father Nikodim and tell him all about it. 'Father Nikodim,' I shall say, 'graciously excuse me, but she is a witch.' 'Why so?' 'Hmm! Do you want to know why?' 'Certainly. . . .' And I shall tell him. And woe to you, woman! Not only at the dread Seat of Judgment, but in your earthly life you'll be punished, too! It's not for nothing there are prayers in the breviary against your kind!"

Suddenly there was a knock at the window, so loud and unusual that Savély turned pale and almost dropped backwards with fright. His wife jumped up, and she, too, turned pale.

"For God's sake, let us come in and get warm!" they heard in a trembling deep bass. "Who lives here? For mercy's sake! We've lost our way."

"Who are you?" asked Raïssa, afraid to look at the window.

"The post," answered a second voice.

"You've succeeded with your devil's tricks," said Savély with a wave of his hand. "No mistake; I am right! Well, you'd better look out!"

The sexton jumped onto the bed in two skips, stretched himself on the feather mattress, and sniffing angrily, turned with his face to the wall. Soon he felt a draft of cold air on his back. The door creaked and the tall figure of a man, plastered over with snow from head to foot, appeared in the doorway. Behind him could be seen a second figure as white.

"Am I to bring in the bags?" asked the second in a hoarse bass voice.

"You can't leave them there." Saying this, the first figure began untying his hood, but gave it up, and pulling it off impatiently with his cap, angrily flung it near the stove. Then taking off his greatcoat, he threw that down beside it, and, without saying good evening, began pacing up and down the hut.

He was a fair-haired, young postman wearing a shabby uniform and black rusty-looking high boots. After warming himself by walking to and fro, he sat down at the table, stretched out his muddy feet towards the sacks, and leaned his chin on his fist. His pale face, reddened in places by the cold, still bore vivid traces of the pain and terror he had just been through. Though distorted by anger and bearing traces of recent suffering, physical and moral, it was handsome in spite of the melting snow on the eyebrows, mustaches, and short beard.

"It's a dog's life!" muttered the postman, looking around the walls and seeming hardly able to believe that he was in the warmth. "We were nearly lost! If it had not been for your light, I don't know what would have happened. Goodness only knows when it will all be over! There's no end to this dog's life! Where have we come?" he asked, dropping his voice and raising his eyes to the sexton's wife.

"To the Gulyaevsky Hill on General Kalinovsky's estate," she answered, startled and blushing.

"Do you hear, Stepan?" The postman turned to the driver, who was wedged in the doorway with a huge mail bag on his shoulders. "We've got to Gulyaevsky Hill."

"Yes . . . we're a long way out." Jerking out these words like a hoarse sigh, the driver went out and soon after returned with another bag, then went out once more and this time brought the postman's sword on a big belt, of the pattern of that long flat blade with which Judith is portrayed by the bedside of Holofernes in cheap woodcuts. Laying the bags along the wall, he went out into the outer room, sat down there, and lighted his pipe.

"Perhaps you'd like some tea after your journey?" Raïssa inquired.

"How can we sit drinking tea?" said the postman, frowning. "We must make haste and get warm, and then set off, or we shall be late for the mail train. We'll stay ten minutes and then get on our way. Only be so good as to show us the way."

"What an infliction it is, this weather!" sighed Raïssa.

"Hmm, yes. . . . Who may you be?"

"We? We live here, by the church. . . . We belong to the clergy. . . . There lies my husband. Savély, get up and say good evening! This used to be a separate parish till eighteen months ago. Of course, when the gentry lived here there were more people, and it was worthwhile to have the services. But now the gentry have gone, and I need not tell you there's nothing for the clergy to live on. The nearest village is Markovka, and that's over three miles away. Savély is on the retired list now, and has got the watchman's job; he has to look after the church. . . ."

And the postman was immediately informed that if Savély were to go to the General's lady and ask her for a letter to the bishop, he would be given a good berth. "But he doesn't go to the General's lady because he is lazy and afraid of people. We belong to the clergy all the same . . ." added Raïssa.

"What do you live on?" asked the postman.

"There's a kitchen garden and a meadow belonging to the church. Only we don't get much from that," sighed Raïssa. "The old skinflint, Father Nikodim, from the next village celebrates here on St. Nicolas' Day in the winter and on St. Nicolas' Day in the summer, and for that he takes almost all the crops for himself. There's no one to stick up for us!"

"You are lying," Savély growled hoarsely. "Father Nikodim is a saintly soul, a luminary of the Church; and if he does take it, it's the regulation!"

"You've a cross one!" said the postman, with a grin. "Have you been married long?"

"It was three years ago the last Sunday before Lent. My father was sexton here in the old days, and when the time came for him to die, he went to the Consistory and asked them to send some unmarried man to marry me that I might keep the place. So I married him."

"Aha, so you killed two birds with one stone!" said the postman, looking at Savély's back. "Got wife and job together."

Savély wriggled his leg impatiently and moved closer to the wall. The postman moved away from the table, stretched, and sat down on the mail bag. After a moment's thought he squeezed the bags with his hands, shifted his sword to the other side, and lay down with one foot touching the floor.

"It's a dog's life," he muttered, putting his hands behind his head and closing his eyes. "I wouldn't wish a wild Tatar such a life."

Soon everything was still. Nothing was audible except the sniffing of Savély and the slow, even breathing of the sleeping postman, who uttered a deep prolonged "h-h-h" at every breath. From time to time there was a sound like a creaking wheel in his throat, and his twitching foot rustled against the bag.

Savély fidgeted under the quilt and looked around slowly. His wife was sitting on the stool, and with her hands pressed against her cheeks was gazing at the postman's face. Her face was immovable, like the face of someone frightened and astonished.

"Well, what are you gaping at?" Savély whispered angrily.

"What is it to you? Lie down!" answered his wife, without taking her eyes off the flaxen head.

Savély angrily puffed all the air out of his chest and turned abruptly to the wall. Three minutes later he turned over restlessly again, knelt up on the bed, and with his hands on the pillow looked askance at his wife. She was still sitting motionless, staring at the visitor. Her cheeks were pale and her eyes were glowing with a strange fire. The sexton cleared his throat, crawled on his stomach off the bed, and going up to the postman, put a handkerchief over his face.

"What's that for?" asked his wife.

"To keep the light out of his eyes."

"Then put out the light!"

Savély looked distrustfully at his wife, put out his lips towards the lamp, but at once thought better of it and clasped his hands.

"Isn't that devilish cunning?" he exclaimed. "Ah! Is there any creature slyer than womankind?"

"Ah, you long-skirted devil!" hissed his wife, frowning with vexation. "You wait a bit!"

And settling herself more comfortably, she stared at the postman again.

It did not matter to her that his face was covered. She was not so much interested in his face as in his whole appearance, in the novelty of this man. His chest was broad and powerful, his hands were slender and well formed, and his graceful, muscular legs were much comelier than Savély's stumps. There could be no comparison, in fact.

"Though I am a long-skirted devil," Savély said after a brief interval, "they've no business to sleep here. . . . It's government work; we shall have to answer for keeping them. If you carry the letters, carry them, you can't go to sleep. . . . Hey! you!" Savély shouted into the outer room. "You, driver. . . . What's your name? Shall I show you the way? Get up; postmen mustn't sleep!"

And Savély, thoroughly roused, ran up to the postman and tugged him by the sleeve.

"Hey, Your Honor, if you must go, go; and if you don't, it's not the thing. . . . Sleeping won't do."

The postman jumped up, sat down, looked with blank eyes around the hut, and lay down again.

"But when are you going?" Savély pattered away. "That's

what the post is for—to get there in good time, do you hear? I'll
take you."

The postman opened his eyes. Warmed and relaxed by his first
sweet sleep, and not yet quite awake, he saw as through a mist
the white neck and the immovable, alluring eyes of the sexton's
wife. He closed his eyes and smiled as though he had been dreaming it all.

"Come, how can you go in such weather!" He heard a soft
feminine voice. "You ought to have a sound sleep and it would do
you good!"

"And what about the post?" said Savély anxiously. "Who's
going to take the post? Are you going to take it, pray, you?"

The postman opened his eyes again, looked at the play of the
dimples on Raïssa's face, remembered where he was, and understood Savély. The thought that he had to go out into the cold
darkness sent a chill shudder all down him, and he winced.

"I might sleep another five minutes," he said, yawning. "I shall
be late, anyway. . . ."

"We might be just in time," came a voice from the outer room.
"All days are not alike; the train may be late for a bit of luck."

The postman got up, and stretching lazily began putting on
his coat.

Savély positively neighed with delight when he saw his visitors
were getting ready to go.

"Give us a hand," the driver shouted to him as he lifted up a
mail bag.

The sexton ran out and helped him drag the post bags into the
yard. The postman began undoing the knot in his hood. The
sexton's wife gazed into his eyes, and seemed trying to look right
into his soul.

"You ought to have a cup of tea . . ." she said.

"I wouldn't say no . . . but, you see, they're getting ready," he
assented. "We are late, anyway."

"Do stay," she whispered, dropping her eyes and touching him
by the sleeve.

The postman got the knot undone at last and flung the hood over his elbow, hesitating. He felt it comfortable standing by Raïssa.

"What a . . . neck you've got! . . ." And he touched her neck with two fingers. Seeing that she did not resist, he stroked her neck and shoulders.

"I say, you are . . ."

"You'd better stay . . . have some tea."

"Where are you putting it?" The driver's voice could be heard outside. "Lay it crossways."

"You'd better stay. . . . Hark how the wind howls."

And the postman, not yet quite awake, not yet quite able to shake off the intoxicating sleep of youth and fatigue, was suddenly overwhelmed by a desire for the sake of which mail bags, postal trains . . . and all things in the world, are forgotten. He glanced at the door in a frightened way, as though he wanted to escape or hide himself, seized Raïssa around the waist, and was just bending over the lamp to put out the light, when he heard the tramp of boots in the outer room, and the driver appeared in the doorway. Savély peeped in over his shoulder. The postman dropped his hands quickly and stood still as though irresolute.

"It's all ready," said the driver. The postman stood still for a moment, resolutely threw up his head as though waking up completely, and followed the driver out. Raïssa was left alone.

"Come, get in and show us the way!" she heard.

One bell sounded languidly, then another, and the jingling notes in a long delicate chain floated away from the hut.

When little by little they had died away, Raïssa got up and nervously paced to and fro. At first she was pale, then she flushed all over. Her face was contorted with hate, her breathing was tremulous, her eyes gleamed with wild, savage anger, and pacing up and down as in a cage, she looked like a tigress menaced with red-hot iron. For a moment she stood still and looked at her abode. Almost half of the room was filled up by the bed, which stretched the length of the whole wall and consisted of a dirty

feather bed, coarse gray pillows, a quilt, and nameless rags of
various sorts. The bed was a shapeless ugly mass which suggested
the shock of hair that always stood up on Savély's head whenever
it occurred to him to oil it. From the bed to the door that led into
the cold outer room stretched the dark stove surrounded by pots
and hanging clouts. Everything, including the absent Savély himself, was dirty, greasy, and smutty to the last degree, so that it
was strange to see a woman's white neck and delicate skin in such
surroundings.

Raïssa ran up to the bed, stretched out her hands as though she
wanted to fling it all about, stamp it underfoot, and tear it to
shreds. But then, as though frightened by contact with the dirt,
she leapt back and began pacing up and down again.

When Savély returned two hours later, worn out and covered
with snow, she was undressed and in bed. Her eyes were closed,
but from the slight tremor that ran over her face he guessed that
she was not asleep. On his way home he had vowed inwardly to
wait till next day and not to touch her, but he could not resist a
biting taunt at her.

"Your witchery was all in vain: he's gone off," he said, grinning
with malignant joy.

His wife remained mute, but her chin quivered. Savély undressed slowly, clambered over his wife, and lay down next to
the wall.

"Tomorrow I'll let Father Nikodim know what sort of wife you
are!" he muttered, curling himself up.

Raïssa turned her face to him and her eyes gleamed.

"The job's enough for you, and you can look for a wife in the
forest, blast you!" she said. "I am no wife for you, a clumsy lout,
a slugabed, God forgive me!"

"Come, come . . . go to sleep!"

"How miserable I am!" sobbed his wife. "If it weren't for you,
I might have married a merchant or some gentleman! If it weren't
for you, I should love my husband now! And you haven't been

buried in the snow, you haven't been frozen on the highroad, you Herod!"

Raïssa cried for a long time. At last she drew a deep sigh and was still. The storm still raged without. Something wailed in the stove, in the chimney, outside the walls, and it seemed to Savély that the wailing was within him, in his ears. This evening had completely confirmed him in his suspicions about his wife. He no longer doubted that his wife, with the aid of the Evil One, controlled the winds and the post sledges. But to add to his grief, this mysteriousness, this supernatural, weird power gave the woman beside him a peculiar, incomprehensible charm of which he had not been conscious before. The fact that in his stupidity he unconsciously threw a poetic glamour over her made her seem, as it were, whiter, sleeker, more unapproachable.

"Witch!" he muttered indignantly. "Tfoo, horrid creature!"

Yet, waiting till she was quiet and began breathing evenly, he touched her head with his finger . . . held her thick plait in his hand for a minute. She did not feel it. Then he grew bolder and stroked her neck.

"Leave off!" she shouted, and prodded him on the nose with her elbow with such violence that he saw stars before his eyes.

The pain in his nose was soon over, but the torture in his heart remained.

Rivkala's Ring

by

SPALDING GRAY

If there is something comforting—religious, if you want—about paranoia, there is still also antiparanoia, where nothing is connected to anything, a condition not many of us can bear for long.

—THOMAS PYNCHON

"Go, go, go," said the bird: "Human kind cannot bear very much reality."

—T. S. ELIOT

CHARACTERS

A PERSON

Now, just some thoughts about the staging of this. I see the character as a kind of manic-y paranoid person who's spinning off these kind of paranoid delusions, trying to make order out of a very frightening and chaotic existence. So I see it fashioned after my character, the character of Spalding Gray that I do in the monologues. And I suggest as a character study, for whoever's playing this, that they see the monologue *47 Beds*, which can be seen at the Lincoln Center Library for the Performing Arts. They'll set up a screen there in the video room if you call them. So that monologue should be observed as a kind of character study. Then, I see the set as quite simple. It's a series of very small surfaces, like, not even platforms—they're too small. They're two-by-two facets like a diamond so the person who's doing the monologue can't get any footing. They're shiny wood, like a wood floor. But he can never, it's always like he's . . . the heel's trying to get his footing. He or she, I don't know. And I guess it's a man, I see a man. And I also see him standing with a microphone, a roving microphone, like a phone on a wire. So that it's amplified. And he's like a stand-up comedian, but in no way working like one—it's reminiscent of one. And the character's barefoot, he's got white pants and one of those real bright Hawaiian-type California shirts. A flowery silk Hawaiian shirt.

And a man tan on his face. His arms look white. Nothing on that but his face is out of show tanning, or actual tan. And behind him, just to his right and about twelve feet back, is a big Venetian blind which is just extended and a little bit opened, and besides general lighting or specific light on him, there is moonlight, blue light that is seeping through the blinds, coming directly and very intense from backstage through that blind. And that's really simply the set, and it's a pretty direct delivery to the audience.

THE PERSON: The day the Chekhov short story arrived I saw my first missing child. On a milk carton. And found a drowned rat in our pool. The photo of the child barely left an impression; it was like any black-and-white photograph of any child anywhere. The more I studied the face, the more it broke up and blended into abstract dots; and besides, I hadn't seen any stray children in the neighborhood. I hadn't seen any children. For that matter, I hadn't seen any people either. There were plenty of houses, but no people. Renée and I were subletting in the Hollywood Hills just below the Hollywood sign. And all the Venetian blinds in all the houses were always closed. And everyone seemed deep dark inside, writing final drafts of their latest TV scripts. Our swimming pool was bigger than our apartment. And much colder. It wasn't heated and we could only look at it and never go in.

Anyway, the particular morning the Chekhov short story arrived, I was on my way to fetch the mail when I noticed the drowned rat floating in among the eucalyptus leaves. The wind had blown wild the night before. A mighty Santa Ana had swept in under a full moon, turning everything upside down. Electricity was blown out and semitrailers were overturned in the lowlands. I couldn't sleep. The wind came in and stirred me and reminded me so much, too much, of raw indifferent nature. The bare-boned breath of the desert whipping in over this crazy glitter town.

So maybe the rat had blown out of the palm tree. Joe, our upstairs neighbor, said that the rats lived in palm trees and that they often drowned in the pool because they were too stupid to use the steps. Or more like their little feet didn't go down that deep. Joe said that when the weather got real hot, all the various creatures came down early out of the Hollywood Hills to take a dip in the pool: coyotes, raccoons, and skunks—all sorts of stuff. And they had the good sense to use the steps of the pool, swim a few measured laps, and then jog back into the hills where they belonged. I pictured a possum in little Nike jogging shoes shaking off the water from his fur and jogging off toward the Hollywood sign.

But I couldn't help calling Renée's attention to this drowned rat—the way it hung there so suspended in the pool with his little legs dangling and his white whiskers out, fully suspended in the water—like it was still alive, or stuffed. Like Mr. Rat, you know, like Mr. Comic Book Rat. Mr. Unharmful Stuffed Rat. The way the water held those whiskers out made me call out to Renée: "Renée! Come quick, come quickly, you've got to see this!"

And she, having no idea what I was talking about, scurried out like a little kid. Scurried out barefoot with her hands clasped across her chest like this little excited kid. And then when she saw what it was, she started screaming and said, "Get it out! Get the net. Get it out!" She couldn't look at it.

It wasn't that I was trying to torture Renée. It was more like a piece of me was missing; the screaming part was missing. Like Renée always said, "I love you but you're a funny guy because you have a piece of your pie missing. Sometimes you don't react in a normal human way to stuff that needs a scream or a cry." And then she does it for me. So Renée completes me, you see. She makes up for the missing piece of the pie. I needed her to be upset about the rat. Then and only then could I toss that sad swollen rat body into the rotten palm leaves and have done with it.

There was another rat, come to think of it. There was another rat in our life in New York City just before we moved to Hollywood. But first, let me tell you what was happening out here just before the Chekhov story came.

Renée and I had just eaten at the Japanese place that night. I had become overly addicted to eating at the Sizzler. And Renée was probably right—it was no good for me. Because I have no boundaries. And so I never get any real satisfaction from those "all you can eat" places. I overdo it and don't get any satisfaction. I feel I have to try everything. And no one says "Stop" or "Pay me more." All the people are so fat. So Renée insisted that we go to this skinny Japanese place that she couldn't get into the week before because it was too crowded. But this time we got in. And it was like we had all of a sudden flown into Japan. I mean, we were the only non-Japanese in the place. And it was real crowded with all these Japanese-speaking Japanese and I felt real uneasy at first. I mean, I felt a little guilty about the bomb and all, even though I was only four years old when we dropped it. But still, I was from Rhode Island, which is still one of the few states in the U.S.A. which celebrates V-J day. But I started to relax a little after a few sakis and some beer and I must admit I felt better being in a place where the service of the food was under tight control. And it all came to us in little frames. And you had plenty of time to meditate on what you ate after you ate it. And lots of time to meditate before you ate. I mean, in short, it was all very controlled (and well framed).

When Renée and I left the restaurant the Santa Ana winds had already begun to blow and we went back to what we were calling home that month to watch our rented TV, which didn't get very good reception because of the Hollywood Hills. But anyway, the important thing (at least I think it was the important thing) was that I turned on the TV and there was this show about General MacArthur taking over Japan after World War II. I had no idea that this had happened. I mean, he became more powerful and more respected than the Emperor of Japan. And also he knew how to deal with the communists. He had all this super faith in democracy, so he just gave the communists total freedom. And they lost. They lost in the elections.

And I said, "Renée, Renée, look. Isn't it strange. Isn't it strange that we should have just eaten in a Japanese restaurant and now this is on TV?" I wanted to say "Jap" restaurant, but I corrected myself. "Look! When we come home and we find this on television—don't you think it's at all strange?"

She said no, she didn't think it was all that strange. She was thinking of other things and went to bed early.

I tried to go to bed after the MacArthur show but I couldn't sleep because of the wind and the full moon. And I got up to watch the late news, which is for me a kind of homeopathic medicine. If I can't sleep because of anxiety, I seek a more anxious state outside of myself. And that is almost always the late news. And that particular night was as good as any other. It was, shall we say, consistent.

It all started with a local report from Laguna Beach with what seems to be an AIDS epidemic there. They had more cases of AIDS relative to the population than in any other city in the United States. And they were having a town meeting to discuss the problem. It was a real alarming sort of thing. This guy, I don't know whether he was a doctor or what, but he was talking about how the number of AIDS cases in the United States had doubled every nine months, and if it continued at that rate, and spread into the general population, that would mean in twelve years everyone in the United States will have been killed. In another twelve years, that's twenty-four years, the population of the world would have been killed ten times over.

Now this doctor-type guy went on to talk about these weird things which I thought were pretty far out for the late news. He said the job of our immune system was to tell the difference between what was itself and what was not itself. You know, to make frames—draw boundaries. And if the immune system gets overworked, it gets overaggressive in response. It gets all confused and the body begins to attack its own cells in a state of what they call "organic paranoia."

It's all led me to believe that eating at the Sizzler was bad because it fostered a lack of definition, a kind of dietary anarchy. Also, I felt that living in Hollywood was bad for the same reasons. Hollywood was the town where everyone came to proliferate their image. And I thought that cancer could be a common disease among movie stars because the image was proliferating out of control and their cells were reacting to that. But finally it all had to do with Russia, I was sure. With Russia or America's attitude toward Russia or Russia's attitude toward America. Just relationshipal problems, big superpowers. And I began to think we were all going to die because of Star Wars. Because that's a massive external defense and no one's putting money into internal body defense. The more that goes to protecting the outside, the less that goes to protecting the inside. External, internal—it's all the same. And also these doctor-type guys no longer know what a high-risk area is. You know, high-risk for AIDS. Everything is high-risk. You never know what the right or wrong place is. I mean, everyone is dying right after they're born, in the sense that we are all headed for an eventual death that will most likely last forever. And it's that "forever" that wipes me out. I mean, wipes me right out. When I think about "forever" it pushes me right out of the existing now because "forever" is so big that it crowds me out, out of the picture. And makes me disappear. And I don't know if or when I'm in a high-risk area for AIDS because it's all a big chain of events that has to be looked at in context from a big kind of overview. And who has that? Who has an overview, right? Because to be over it, to have an overview is to be outside of it. And no one can get out. We're all in too deep.

Well, during this whole report on AIDS, the AIDS epidemic in Laguna, I got up and took this big dose of folic acid, which is supposed to help hold your cell walls together. And while I was in the kitchen, this ad came on the TV for the Doggery Boutique. And it showed clips of this woman holding a poodle down in a Jacuzzi. The poodle looked very disturbed and was trying to get out, but it was helpless. I thought about the drowned rat in the pool and I got up to make some warm milk and take a big dose of L-Tryptophan, a natural tranquilizer made from turkey enzymes. A guy sold it to me in a health food store in Venice—I bought six jars of it on sale. He was a good salesman: He said, "Ever wonder why you want to go right to sleep after a big Christmas dinner?"

And that stopped me, because it was true. Thinking back over it, that was a major memory of Christmas and Thanksgiving. You know—sleeping. And I just thought it had to do with eating too much, and he said, "No, no, no, it had to do with L-Tryptophan in the turkey." Then he tried to sell me six jars of something. I can't remember the name of it. It was for aiding the memory. Um. And I told him I didn't want to remember anymore, it was too painful. That I just wanted to relax, and go out simple.

Then he starts on this whole rap how history not remembered is doomed to repeat itself.

And I fled from the store, only to pass this guy with a

shopping cart out on the street, and it was all filled with his possessions. And he calls out to me, saying, "Fifty dollars to bring democracy back to the United States!"

And that stops me. I mean, anyone who has the balls to ask for a fifty-dollar handout . . . well, anyway, I stopped and I say, "Tell me, when did democracy leave America?"

And he says, "Nineteen sixty-three, when the wealthy right wing paid for all those assassination plots."

And I listened because the guy started to make disturbing sense, until I asked him, "What can we do about this, I mean, where is the fifty dollars gonna go? And if I give you fifty dollars, where's it gonna go?"

And he says, "To organize the big July 22nd rally."

"Really? What rally?"

He says, "What's gonna save us all is that Christ and Moses are both coming back on July 22nd. Together they're coming back. What a team!"

I said, "Where's this all going to happen?"

"Right here!" he says. "On the beach of Venice. Where else could we hold that many people?"

So I said, "Okay, would fifty cents help?"

And he said, "Yeah, thanks. Anything, anything will help."

And just as we were talking, you know, about Jesus and Moses coming back, this real wasted bum, barefoot, an old hippie with a bandana wrapped around his head, comes wandering through and says, "Hey I'm Jesus, I'm Jesus Christ!"

And the guy with the shopping cart says, "Keep moving, Jack, don't bug me with that crazy shit!"

And I think: Where does it all stop? Where does it all begin? It's like panning for gold. But no one knows what the gold is anymore. I mean, that's what I said to Renée when we made up our minds to come out to Hollywood. I said, "That's where the gold is. That's where the money is. Just pretend we're pioneers. It's like panning for gold."

. . .

So we get this cheap flight out on Tower Air, and I'm feeling real nervous because it's cheap. And I'm worried that the pilot isn't getting paid enough money to make him satisfied, and so he's in a rush and we're sitting there, and behind us are these two dark, sensual ladies. And one of them moves in on a guy in front of us because he's real cute. And he's got one of those mod-punk haircuts that ends in a sort of long rattail that goes out over his collar. And there's an empty seat next to him and it looks like she's plying him with lines of coke. You know, cocaine! And, I mean, she's just making little lines of cocaine on the dinner tray, and after a few snorts, they disappear into the toilet to join the mile-high club. And they're in there for a long time and this long line begins to build up outside the toilet. And I'm amazed and jealous that they don't seem to care. Their pleasure is more important than anyone else's needs. It must be the drug, I think. I rarely take the stuff; it's too expensive, and too up and down—but I never say no to an offered snort (which is rare).

The last time I had it was when my friend George came out to visit from the West Coast. Oh, that was incredible that day. That was the day we saw all that money blowing in the street.

Every time my friend George comes from the Coast for a visit he wants to go with me to a place in New York where I haven't been for a long time. I guess he wants us to be experiential equals, you know, on equal ground. So this particular spring day we wound up in the East Village, corner of 11th and B, to be precise. And the vibes are pretty heavy; they're as heavy as they've ever been. And George gets queasy because he's got two hundred dollars in cash in his pocket. And he wants to move on and I say, "Let's go over to Surprising SoHo." And we get there, and we're walking down West Broadway, which is really crowded with all these tourists and bridge and tunnel people. You know, wall-to-wall mink. And the first scene that George and I come upon is this silver-gray Cadillac with chrome wheels. And it's talking. The car is talking, or rather, it's crying out, "BURGLAR! BURGLAR! BURGLAR! BURGLAR!" Over and over again, "BURGLAR! BURGLAR! BURGLAR!" And all these women in their minks and foxes are standing around staring at this car which is talking. And they're all looking at it as if to say, "Who, me? Who you calling a burglar? ME?!" And the car is just sitting there like this . . . you know, like this big accusatory metal beast, just sitting there going "BURGLAR! BURGLAR!"

So George and I take this all in and move on down a little farther to the corner of Spring Street and West Broadway, where we come upon this crowd of people all standing around in a circle looking down like they're looking into a great hole in the Earth. Like they're looking into El Dorado. Like the Earth has opened up and they're looking at this gold city. And one woman is crying out, "What shall we do? What shall we do!" And we get to the circle and look down and see green not gold, but green instead of gold. There's all this green money blowing in the wind in circles like leaves. I mean, there must have been a thousand dollars there! I saw some hundreds, lots of fifties, uncountable twenties. And all the people are standing around it. And it's blowing in circles. And not one person is going in for it—but George.

As soon as George sees that money he just follows his natural inclinations and he bends down and picks up a twenty. Just one twenty out of all that money, he just picks up one twenty.

And the woman who has been crying out, "What shall we do? What shall we do?" turns to him and says, "Oh, my God! What are you doing?"

And George looks right back at her and says, "You know what I'm doing." And we walk off down the street.

And as we're walking, I say, "George, why didn't you pick up a hundred? Why did you pick up a twenty?"

And he goes, "What? There were hundreds there?" And then he stops, looks back, and then he turns to me and says, "No. That would be greed, wouldn't it?" And then we move off down the street together.

Now I can't stop thinking about that money. It's become one of those "spots" that are forever marked in the city. No matter how much I try to be here now and see the spot for what it is, I can't get that blowing money out of my mind.

It's the same with the spot on North Moore and Greenwich where Renée and I saw the fresh body of a blond woman. She must have jumped just minutes before we rounded the corner. And it was such a nice day. It was spring and a Sunday. And the streets were empty and we saw these people standing around this blond body. She was so . . . dead. So there, but so not there. I mean, there wasn't one hint of life coming off of her. Her face was white like wax, in a puddle of blood. The blood flowed out from some opening, some crack somewhere that you couldn't see. And her whole body was sprawled in an impossible sprawl. A fix of wasted limbs nobody could imitate. And she had only jumped from the fifth-floor window. That's all! That's as high as the building was—just five stories.

Renée burst into tears and ran away. She had had bad luck with suicides in that neighborhood before. Just the past winter when she was going over to apply for an apartment at Independence Plaza, some woman jumped from about twenty stories up, bounced off a trash dumpster, and broke open at Renée's feet like an overripe watermelon. So I could understand why she didn't stick around.

I stuck around because I couldn't see it. I mean, at first it was so strange, I had to look hard so I could see it. And all the time there was this old woman who lived on the fourth floor of the building and she was standing over that body. And the face was so white. And the blond hair was so beautiful that I wanted to run my hands through it and cry. And the blood was so red, so crimson. How could someone else's death look so beautiful? I kept wondering. And this old woman was standing over the body. This old woman with a kind of shaky palsy. She was shaking all over and saying over and over again, "How could she have done it? She's so beautiful and young." And she doesn't even know who this dead body is! And the other people are talking about how the dead body was a woman who was just crashing there, just visiting. And she couldn't sleep, she was real upset. She had a rough night. And her friends had stayed up with her all night. They had done an all-night vigil to help her keep it together. And then around morning she seemed better and the friends had dozed off like Christ's disciples. You can't blame them. And she did it. She just jumped. And here was this old woman who felt from her side of the fence that beauty was enough to go on living for. You could just live for sheer beauty, physical beauty. Why would anyone who had that kind of beauty, who possessed that kind of beauty, why would they want to jump? She couldn't understand it.

I stayed and watched until the ambulance came. I wanted to see how they would deal with the body. Who would finally touch it. And how they would touch it. But no one touched it. The ambulance came and they had a stretcher that was like a scoop. The stretcher opened and then closed like a big mouth eating the body whole. It just scooped it up like this very, very dead thing that it was. And the blood stayed in a big puddle, and a gust of wind came off the river and blew a fine layer of city dirt over the blood and the blood turned a deep darker dirty red. And it left a stain that stayed for months. And now it's just the old dirty sidewalk again.

But every time I walk over it, I see that body. Just like I

see the money blowing every time I walk by that corner of Spring Street and West Broadway.

Anyway, a Sizzler ad comes on the TV and I realize why I'm addicted to Sizzler—they have such great ads. And the food looks so good. And they follow the ad with this outrageous story about a man, a photographer in Florida, who has gotten cancer of the eye. And I think: Oh my good Christ, that's enough! You know, just that: that's enough of the story right there. I mean, you could end it all right there. But they didn't. They went on to describe this horrible medical mistake. It turns out that in order to operate on his eye, they had to remove some of his spinal fluid to take some of the pressure off his eye. And instead of putting his spinal fluid back into his spine, they inject him with some sort of embalming fluid which just happened to be in the operating room in an unmarked bottle. And they end up embalming the patient. I mean, they turn him into a vegetable. And they've got the doctor on television testifying. The doctor who did this. And he's right there on TV saying he can't begin to say how sorry he is. Now there's nothing left for me to turn to.

I'm thinking of opening a bottle of brandy when this fantastic, redemptive piece of news comes on about a Chinese 747 which was on its way from China to L.A.; and all of the sudden it just drops out of the sky. It just starts to fall. It falls twenty-nine thousand feet just like that. It was only thirty seconds and a thousand feet away from plunging into the Pacific Ocean when the pilot suddenly brings it out of its plunge.

Now there is a man I'd like to meet—that pilot. And the words of one of those new-age positive thinkers come back to me. He's got a retreat in Hawaii, I forget his name. And he's always saying, "When you meet reality, you do one of three things: you fight it, you flee it, or you flow." And by "flow," I figure he means embrace your fears. That's how I interpret it. And that's a thought. That's the other side of paranoia, or the other side of antiparanoia. Somewhere in between. It's the middle way, to embrace the fear. That's what that pilot must have done with the last thousand feet. He must have put his arms around fear and gotten clear.

So I just turned off the TV and sat there and listened to the sound of the wind fill up the room. And I looked down at the brick hearth of the little fireplace that we couldn't use because the chimney needed cleaning. And all the smoke filled the room. And I looked down to see a copy of *Vanity Fair* with Diane Keaton dressed all in white smiling back. And then I looked up at the wall at this reproduction of this nineteenth-century painting of this ship sailing in a storm off the white cliffs of Dover. And that Matthew Arnold poem came back to me. That line. Through my head it went like a ticker tape. The line, you know, over and over was something like "Ah love, let us be true to one another. Ah love, let us be true." And I turned out the lights and watched the full moon as it flashed through the ripping palm trees and the spaces in the Venetian blind.

And I remembered that other rat—the one on Halloween back in New York City. By mistake I had cracked a shaving mirror and I was real upset because it was Halloween and I was afraid of seven years' bad luck. And then, when I was coming home at night, actually, coming to Renée's loft, which was one of many homes then, I was starting up the steps and I sensed kind of scrambling energy coming from under one of those steps in front of me. Now it's not as though I was not on the lookout for evil or death in those halls, but I had always expected it to take a human form—two big men coming at me with a knife. I just never expected it to be this. And out from under the seventh step, this huge brown city rat jumped onto my chest. And I fell back and let out with an involuntary yell. I just went "AHHHHHHH. . . ." And then I remembered the old saying "Never corner a rat" and I began running in circles so as not to corner him. And the rat must have heard the old saying about never corner a human being because it also ran in circles. And I was beating it with my raincoat. Beating it off, and we ran around and around till somehow the rat disappeared. It went away.

Now I knew I should have kept that whole event to myself. You know, just held on to it. I should have kept it as a secret—embraced my fear. You know, reprocess it, and not report it to Renée or any woman for that matter. You know, be like Christ. You know how Christ would take on evil stuff. He would take it on him, not pass it along. Like he had some sort of charcoal filter system in his psyche which enabled him to filter out evil karma or responses to it. Like a lobster. It's funny but I've always thought of Christ as a lobster. When I eat lobster I feel more like I'm eating the body of Christ because a lobster crawls on the bottom of the ocean and eats all this dead stuff, it eats garbage. It eats shit. And then it converts it all into this pure sweet white meat. And that's like Christ to me. He doesn't pass it on. And holding on to it doesn't cause cancer. Or maybe it would have if he had lived past thirty-three.

But the rat, I was telling you about the rat. Yes, I know where I was. Renée and the rat. Now I know how afraid of rats Renée was, and I could have just not told her what happened to me. You know, absorb it. Keep it to myself. But I didn't. When she called, I said, "Be careful when you come home because this big rat jumped out on my chest."

And she screamed and said, "That's it, I'm not coming home." And she hung up.

After about an hour or so, I hear this wild banging, and

it's Renée coming up the stairs with this big two-by-four. And she's swinging it and smashing the steps and walls and yelling. The rat was long gone by then.

But anyway, some demi-shaman friend of mine who lives upstate said that it would never happen twice. You know, to have a rat jump out on your chest would be like being hit by lightning twice. But the worst of it was that it made me paranoid and ill at ease. I thought it was a kind of black omen—I was sure it had to do with breaking the mirror on Halloween, and the rat was the beginning of seven years' bad luck. And I just didn't think I was ready for it. I was in no way ready for seven years' bad luck. So I came to Renée in the morning and I said, "Help me. What shall I do?"

And with all confidence and no thought about it, she said, "Kneel. Kneel down and kiss my grandmother Rivkala's ring."

This beautiful ring was the only thing that Renée's grandmother had left her. Her grandmother was poor and from Russia. Peasant stock. And she had left Renée this ring. And I wanted to believe in it. I wanted to believe in the power of the ring.

And Renée said, "Kiss the ring, and you'll dispel all bad luck."

And I went down on my knees on the kitchen floor and I kissed the ring. And as I did it, I saw a long bridge of toothless smiles—all Renée's relatives marching out over the world and back to Russia. I saw them standing, smiling in bending wheat fields. And I was relieved. A burden lifted from my mind. And I felt clear again. Something had transpired that I didn't understand, but I knew that the seven years' bad luck had been lifted, or counteracted by Rivkala's ring.

Thinking on this ring I felt sleepy now, and crept into bed with Renée, who was naked and asleep and smelling like horses in a stable. Breathing beside me like the Russian wheat field going down in the summer wind. And I tucked in beside her, and we fit together like spoons. Her warm flesh heaved to adjust to mine, as my belly fit into the curve of her back.

And for one brief instant, we were one as that nuclear wind tore at the palms and split the moon through the Venetian blinds. I closed my eyes to it and saw just before sleep, I saw the last images spin out like a wheel of life and death. All spinning and mixed together. I saw the sacrificial blonde, sprawled, broken in her leaking blood. I saw the wild green money spinning in the wind above her, and above that, high high up, a Chinese 747 was about to fall from the sky. And above all this shedding rays of silver light was that ring. Rivkala's ring. That blessed ring. And beyond that, black black, dark black. Oh dark dark dark, forever dark. We all go into the dark.

Notes

A NOTE ABOUT THE FIRST PRODUCTION

At The Acting Company's world-premiere performance of *Orchards*, given at The Krannert Center for the Performing Arts in Champaign-Urbana, Illinois, on September 19, 1985, the seven plays were staged in the order in which they appear in this book.

The plays were directed by Robert Falls.

Sets designed by Adrianne Lobel. Costumes designed by Laura Crow. Lights designed by Paul Gallo. Original music by Louis Rosen. Dramaturg: Anne Cattaneo. Assistant Director: Rob Bundy. Production Stage Manager: Maureen F. Gibson. Stage Manager: Susan B. Feltman.

The casts were as follows:

The Man in a Case by Wendy Wasserstein

BYELKINOV	Brian Reddy
VARINKA	Mariangela Pino

Vint by David Mamet

PORTER	Craig Bryant
COMMISSIONER PERSOLIN	Terrence Caza
ZVISDULIN	Joel F. Miller
KULAKEVITCH	Phil Meyer
NEDKUDOV	Kevin Jackson
PSIULIN	Aled Davies

Drowning by Maria Irene Fornes

PEA	Philip Goodwin
ROE	Anthony Powell
STEPHEN	Mark Moses

A Dopey Fairy Tale by Michael Weller

SMILE	Phil Meyer
FATHER BAKER	Terrence Caza
MOTHER BAKER	Susan Finch
CLARENCE	Craig Bryant
CHATTER (the dog)	Joel F. Miller
MAYOR	Kevin Jackson
MAGISTRATE	Anthony Powell
MINISTER	Mark Moses
FEMALE FROG	Wendy Brennan
MALE FROG	Brian Reddy
SAD PRINCESS GLADYS	Laura Brutsman

Eve of the Trial by Samm-Art Williams

MA LOLA	Susan Finch
LESTER SIMMONS	Brian Reddy
PEARL SIMMONS	Laura Brutsman
TATE	Joel F. Miller
ALEX BUSHKIN	Philip Goodwin
LILLY	Mariangela Pino
KITTY	Wendy Brennan

The Talking Dog by John Guare

F	Susan Finch
M	Mark Moses
HANG-GLIDER #1	Kevin Jackson
HANG-GLIDER #2	Phil Meyer

Rivkala's Ring by Spalding Gray

THE SPEAKER	Aled Davies

Maria Irene Fornes is the author of *Promenade*, *The Successful Life of 3*, *Fefu and Her Friends*, *The Danube*, *Mud*, *Sarita*, and *The Conduct of Life*, all of which earned her Obie Awards for writing. She is the recipient of a Guggenheim Fellowship, a Rockefeller Foundation grant, and an award from the American Academy and Institute of Arts and Letters.

Spalding Gray has performed his autobiographical monologues to acclaim throughout the United States—at the Goodman Theater (Chicago), the Mark Taper Forum (Los Angeles), the Walker Art Center (Minneapolis), the Performing Garage and the Mitzi E. Newhouse Theater at Lincoln Center (New York)—as well as in Europe, Canada, and Australia. His 1985 monologue *Swimming to Cambodia* (available in book form) is based on his experiences on the set of *The Killing Fields*, in which he made his motion picture debut. Six of his monologues are collected in the book *Sex and Death to the Age 14*.

John Guare's plays—which include *Gardenia*, *Lydie Breeze*, *Bosoms and Neglect*, *Rich and Famous*, and *The House of Blue Leaves*—have earned him an Award of Merit from the American Academy and Institute of Arts and Letters. He also wrote the screenplay for *Atlantic City* (which won him an Oscar nomination as well as the New York, Los Angeles, and National Film Critics Prize for Best Screenplay) and the book and lyrics for *Two Gentlemen of Verona* (winner of the New York Drama Critics' Circle Award and the Tony Award for Best Musical).

David Mamet was awarded the Pulitzer Prize in 1984 for his play *Glengarry Glen Ross*. He is also the author of *American Buffalo*, *Sexual Perversity in Chicago*, *The Duck Variations*, *Prairie du Chien*, and *The Shawl*, among other plays. His adaptation of Chekhov's *The Cherry Orchard* was produced at the Goodman Theater in Chicago in 1985. His screenplays include *The Postman Always Rings Twice* and *The Verdict*.

Wendy Wasserstein is the author of *Uncommon Women and Others*, *Isn't It Romantic*, *Tender Offer*, and other plays. For the PBS *Great Performances* series she has adapted *Uncommon Women and Others* and John Cheever's story "The Sorrows of Gin." She is the recipient of a Guggenheim Fellowship and a grant from the National Endowment for the Arts.

Michael Weller's plays include *Moonchildren*, *Split*, *Fishing*, *Loose Ends*, *The Ballad of Soapy Smith*, and, most recently, *Ghost on Fire*, which premiered at the La Jolla Playhouse in 1985. He is the author of the screenplays for *Hair* and *Ragtime*.

Samm-Art Williams's play *Home*, produced on Broadway, won the Outer Critics' Circle Award for Best Play and was nominated for a Tony Award in the category of Best Play in 1980. His other plays include *Eyes of the American*, *Welcome to Black River*, *Friends*, *Brass Birds Don't Sing*, *The Sixteenth Round*, and *A Love Play*. He has also written extensively for television, and collaborated on the book of Broadway's *Lena Horne: The Lady and Her Music*.

A NOTE ON THE TYPE

This book was set in a digitized version of Janson. The hot-metal version of Janson was a recutting made direct from type cast from matrices long thought to have been made by the Dutchman Anton Janson, who was a practicing type founder in Leipzig during the years 1668–1687. However, it has been conclusively demonstrated that these types are actually the work of Nicholas Kis (1650–1702), a Hungarian, who most probably learned his trade from the master Dutch type founder Dirk Voskens. The type is an excellent example of the influential and sturdy Dutch types that prevailed in England up to the time William Caslon (1692–1766) developed his own incomparable designs from them.

Composed by Graphic Composition, Inc., Athens, Georgia

Printed and bound by Fairfield Graphics, Fairfield, Pennsylvania

Typography and binding design by Tasha Hall

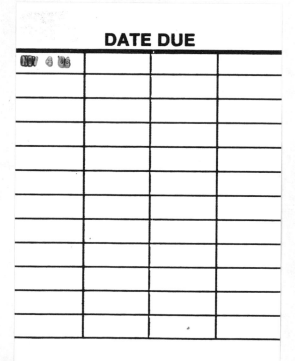

DATE DUE

NOV 4 06			